SHARON A. DAVISON, PH.D.

YOU GO GIRL

START. BUILD. SELL.

FIRST EDITION

Blue Fish Point Publishing

First Edition

Blue Fish Point Publishing
181 Key Deer Boulevard, #231
Big Pine, Florida 33043
USA

Editorial services: LA Communications, LLC
Illustrations: Thomas Troisch
Author's photo: Katya Palladina

You Go Girl: Start. Build. Sell.

Library of Congress Control Number: 2018910669

Printed in the United States of America

Print ISBN 978-1-73256-831-0
eBook ISBN 978-1-73256-835-8

Encouraging

the entrepreneurial spirit

within each of us

Contents

INTRODUCTION ix

CHAPTER 1: **Being a Leader** 1

CHAPTER 2: **From Ideas to Reality** 13

CHAPTER 3: **It Takes a Team** 23

CHAPTER 4: **Inevitable Mistakes** 33

CHAPTER 5: **Those You Trust (including yourself)** 43

CHAPTER 6: **Money Matters** 51

CHAPTER 7: **Marketing and Self-Promotion** 61

CHAPTER 8: **Managing Growth** 71

CHAPTER 9: **Looking and Feeling the Part** 83

CHAPTER 10: **Flexibility is Key** 95

CHAPTER 11: **Creativity and Positive Thinking** 105

CHAPTER 12: **Going Above and Beyond** 115

CHAPTER 13: **Implementing an Exit Plan** 123

CHAPTER 14: **Winning and Losing** 133

AFTERWORD 141

ACKNOWLEDGMENTS 143

ABOUT THE AUTHOR 147

INTRODUCTION

While not everyone is cut out to be an entrepreneur, every-one—both women and men—can benefit from the mind-set and tactics that make a business owner successful. A certain amount of self-confidence is crucial, which creates the ability to take risks, or may even develop after one actually begins a venture.

I wish everyone could know the satisfaction that comes from assuming a risk and having a positive outcome. Inevitably there is fear—of failure, of losing or not making money, of embarrassment, or some other nerve-wracking concern. Sometimes there is even the fear of success, for it brings change, which is always challenging.

Successful entrepreneurs proceed in spite of fears, not because they don't have them. We're all human and no one of us is immune from doubt. Those of us who take risks proceed anyway.

Of course, it's best to take calculated risks. That's what this book is about. I am sharing my observations and conclusions on what I've learned that led to my successfully starting, building and selling a multimillion-dollar business. The lessons are applicable to other situations too, for entrepreneurship is an innovative and pragmatic state of mind as much as it is the creation and management of businesses.

Here's to your present and future ventures. May you be wildly successful beyond your dreams.

– Sharon A. Davison

CHAPTER 1:

Being a Leader

"There are many things that seem impossible only so long as one does not attempt them."—Andre Gide, French author and Nobel Prize winner in literature

"I never dreamed about success. I worked for it."—Estee Lauder, founder of cosmetic empire

The ideal leader

There is no magic formula to what makes a great leader. There are certainly traits that great leaders have in common, but we are all unique. What matters is that each leader continues to seek improvement—continually innovating and anticipating or responding to their customers' or employees' needs in an effective manner.

If you have direct reports, don't expect them to do things you would never do yourself. Leading is best when it is not a power trip.

Remember that leadership is a privilege we earn and should not be taken lightly.

What matters most

The things that matter most about being a leader are vision, mission and values. Mine are simple:

Do great work. Have fun. Make money. Never work with people you don't like. Be honest and be brave.

People want to know where you are heading, what type of ride it will be, and if you care. The one thing I consistently hear from my clients is they know I am a straight shooter. If I say I am going to do something, I do it. That is one of my core values–honesty.

Not everyone wants to hear the truth, but if they ask I am good at laying it out. My mission as a leader is to always leave people in a better place than where they started. My vision is to create a business in which people matter and they are respected. I believe in not focusing on the negative but rather playing off people's strengths.

Thanks, or not

Early on I figured out my mission is to help people get ahead; and when I work with an employee or client, I want the best for him or her. If that means helping that person get a promotion, be recognized or just get out of a tight spot, I'm known for that. It's a great feeling knowing someone is getting ahead because of your help.

A few years ago, one of my former clients called to tell me his daughter was having a hard time finding direction. He said she was clever, motivated and eager to learn but she was just working as a barista after finishing a four-year college degree. Would I consider taking her on as an intern to show her what it is like to work in a creative business?

I agreed to meet her and he was right–his daughter had great potential and so we hired her. She started as an intern and within three months she was an assistant project manager. Within a year she was handling projects on her own. And she found what I do so intriguing–designing software–that she applied for a master's program.

We adjusted her schedule so she could take classes and use the skills she was learning in-house. Once she was done with school though, she did not stay with us. Instead she found a role in a company that focuses exclusively on software design. I could have been upset we invested so much time and effort in her. Instead, I am proud she found her calling.

I ran into my former client the other day and he told me his daughter is doing fantastically. And he thanked me. I thanked him too—for giving me all the work he did and trusting me with his daughter to help her find her passion and then soar.

My former client may end up hiring me in the future or recommending me to another firm. And though not everyone I invest in appreciates what I do for them, at least I know what help and guidance I provide.

In fact, one of the people I helped most ended up resenting me and building a story that did not include me. That's fine too, for knowing when to be indifferent to negative hurtful people is an art in itself—it gives you power when you are able to focus only on the wins and stop feeding the losses.

Good versus bad

I had to remind a client the other day that she was giving a bad apple in her business all the attention and forgetting the shining star she has who really deserves the attention.

It is natural to sometimes try and fix people who are giving us problems while ignoring those who excel. Once you try reversing that attention, the results are amazing.

By all means, give everyone a chance. But if bad behavior keeps repeating, learn to let negative people go.

Friendly, but not too much so

Depending on the size of your staff, you should develop relationships with at least those individuals who are your direct reports. This can be done through lunches, dinners, or company events when you get to know their likes and dislikes.

Of course, this is a job and you don't want to get too close. Still, the more you know about what motivates your team members, the better leader you will become—always, always keeping the best interest of the company in mind.

I was reminded of this when someone with whom I was talking told me how underpaid she felt. Her boss was busy buying all sorts of new things—a car, boat, and taking expensive trips. The employee felt she was entitled to make more of the profits too. Whether or not that was true, she felt resentful and more than a little envious. After all, it is human nature to want what others around us are enjoying.

The woman for whom she works wanted to share her success, so she invited this employee for a ride in the luxury car and an outing on the expensive boat. Her effort to get close backfired with a disgruntled employee.

Keep this story in mind.

Showing up...and on time

My husband Rex and I have a family motto: "We show up." When we are invited to parties, events and functions, we make a point of showing up. There are two reasons. One—it may be an awesome event; and two—we want to show people we appreciate the effort they made to give the event.

In my personal life I tend to be late for things. Rex thinks that if he asks me to hurry up I just take longer. I vehemently deny doing this on purpose! It makes for a lot of good-natured kidding between us.

Since I do tend to be late, in business I try hard to be on time. To accomplish this, I block out time before or after meetings to give myself time for travel or conversations that run over. I also make sure to communicate if for some reason I am running behind. What this has done for me over the years is to give me a reputation for being dependable.

When I didn't get to a meeting, I even heard one person say that something must have happened because it was so unlike me not to show up. I'd gotten the time zone wrong and completely missed the meeting. But I got a pass since it does not happen often.

There is one person with whom I recently started to work. He is always late and sometimes does not show up at all. When this person wants to schedule time with me I don't trust him because I've already gotten burned many times waiting around. My time is not being respected.

Showing up on time tells a lot about someone. Whose time is more important—yours or theirs?

Integrity

Your reputation is one of your most important assets so never share confidential information and don't associate with liars. Also make sure to honor non-disclosure agreements (NDAs).

It's important not to jeopardize your reputation for a couple thousand, or even a couple hundred thousand dollars.

Don't throw anyone under the bus either. If someone does this to you, keep your cool and revel in the knowledge of your own self-worth. Only bullies and cowards put the blame on others instead of taking responsibility.

Top dog

Being called "top dog" or "rock star" is a fantastic feeling. If you are the best at something, customers will come to you without your having to market to them.

I recently got a phone call from a person I didn't know. She wanted me to do a project for her. I asked how she got my name and she told me I am well known for getting things done. Based on that recommendation, she decided I was the one to help her.

I asked who recommended me and she gave me the names of three different people. It seems every time she asked someone for a referral, my name kept coming up. To me that is a great feeling—being "top dog."

All I ever did was deliver what I said I was going to do for the price I said it would take. When something happened that I couldn't meet a goal, I immediately reset expectations with the customer. Obviously, this approach is appreciated and it's given me a good reputation.

It's hard to earn a good reputation. Once you have it, don't squander it. Continue to do what earned you that reputation and if possible, do even more.

Envy versus jealousy

Being envious or being jealous are not great feelings; either one makes you feel less than great. Knowing the difference can help how you interact with people.

Envy is when you want what someone else has. You can envy a friend who may be running a more successful business than yours while wondering what it took her to get there. Or you can feel jealous of this same person for getting projects or accounts you thought should be yours. Envy is when you want what someone has, whereas jealousy is when you think someone is trying, or already succeeded, in taking something that rightfully belongs to you.

Another way to look at the difference is that envy involves only two parties—you and the person with whom you are envious. Jealousy involves three parties—you, the person with whom you are envious, and someone or something else. Envy is a reaction to lacking something. Being jealous is a reaction to the threat of losing something.

I bring this up because envy can be a good thing. It can help you set goals and work toward something you didn't think you could obtain.

Don't give time or effort to jealousy as you don't need to be threatened by others. It's useless to feel that someone else's success takes something away from you.

Envy is a good motivator to consider forming partnerships. If it's not feasible for you to deliver on a project or job, find out who can do the work and send business their way or offer to partner with them. This way, you'll build a reputation as a go-to person. Helping others, even if it does not directly impact you at first, will bring benefits in the long run.

Sailing for sheer enjoyment

I love sailing and several years ago I decided to earn my captain's license. I did this to prove to myself I could conquer the challenge and earn the credential. Like running a business, being captain of a ship is a wonderful metaphor for being in charge.

The combination of my business in Seattle plus my sailboat gave Rex and me the opportunity to branch out and deliver training on team building using the boat.

Every Thursday in the summer, we would also invite employees and clients to join us. It was a way to entertain for business. It was also a way for us to get out on the water, which I love.

At other times, my husband and I would sail—just the two of us.

With the training needed to obtain my license, I learned how to navigate and what to do in a variety of situations. After all, knowing the right thing to do is potentially vital for ensuring the safety of my own life and those of others who may depend on me.

When I bought my 42 foot sailboat, the salesman was terribly sexist. He said, "It's like a young boy buying a Ferrari—who's going to insure you?"

I knew he would never say that to a man so I promptly called up a woman insurance agent. She told me, "I'll insure you to go around the world and through the Panama Canal if you like."

So I got my 42 foot sailboat and took a training class with experienced sea captains. It was definitely a good ol' boys club. But my husband treated me with respect, like always.

However, the instructors treated me with contempt. I would ask questions, which is always a good thing to do. But they wouldn't answer my questions. I haven't ever faced that kind of animosity in business—it's just crazy.

At the time it was a big deal that I was able to obtain my license with all the cards stacked against me.

No such thing as too fast

The next dare I took was to get my motorcycle license and to proudly buy a Harley. Awhile later, my stepson, Jake, returned from a tour in Iraq where he was an air traffic controller for the Army National Guard. He had saved his money and wanted to buy my Harley from me. I agreed.

Then Jake and my husband, Rex, went with me to the Harley Davidson dealer so I could buy myself a new motorcycle. Again I experienced prejudice because I wanted a V-Rod. The salesman told me the bike was too fast and too much for me to handle.

"Why stay away from that?" my husband asked. Both Rex and Jake encouraged me to take a test drive.

On the test drive, I never took it out of third gear—it scared me to death. I was sitting at the light with the engine idling and a man did a double take and said, "Damn girl, that's hot."

I returned to the dealership and immediately told the salesman, "I'll take it."

Later Rex and Jake asked me what changed my mind. I told them, "It just rides nicely! Plus, it makes me look skinny when I drive since it's such a big muscle bike."

Acting like a duck

I do a lot of things that scare the hell out of me. I just won't let that stop me.

I think it's important to do something every day that scares you. I believe in acting like a duck—smooth on the surface and paddling like crazy down below.

It's important to conquer our fears, but not everybody is cut out to be a risk-taker. I personally thrive on conflict but others seek to avoid it. Because of that, I miss owning a business when I'm between businesses. I crave the challenge of setting myself up for financial success.

I'm also afraid of not having enough money because I don't want others to have to take care of me. I don't want to have to rely on anyone else. That's perhaps my greatest fear.

**Appear calm even if you're paddling
like crazy under the surface.**

No regrets

I can point to large sums of money I could have had if I'd made different choices. But I don't dwell on this stuff or kick myself. After all, if you're not making mistakes, you're not doing enough.

I can honestly say I have second-guessed many of my choices, but I don't sit around wishing I could go back.

I love the quote often attributed to Winston Churchill, "If you're going through hell, keep going." I think of it all the time. When things seem like they are not going well or I have taken on too much, I just remember it is not the end game yet but rather just part of the process.

Yes, things get stressful and can be difficult, but the rewards are amazing. Being an entrepreneur or in charge of your own destiny in some other way is definitely worth it. And luckily there have been times when I did make lots of money, so perhaps it balances out.

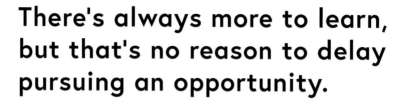

There's always more to learn, but that's no reason to delay pursuing an opportunity.

CHAPTER 2

From Ideas to Reality

"An investment in knowledge pays the best interest."—Benjamin Franklin, inventor, statesman and diplomat

"Focus on a few key objectives … I only have three things to do. I have to choose the right people, allocate the right number of dollars, and transmit ideas from one division to another with the speed of light. So I'm really in the business of being the gatekeeper and the transmitter of ideas."—Jack Welch, retired chairman and CEO of General Electric

Not all ideas are great

We are all guilty of what is called "confirmation bias." I would guess that entrepreneurs are guilty of this more than most.

What happens is you come up with a belief and promptly reject all data or information swirling around you that goes against your belief. Not surprisingly, this is the downfall of many, many companies.

My husband was asked to do some development work for a start-up whose owner was a professional photographer. The start-up entrepreneur was building a company around his skill set and what he saw as a huge need in the industry—he wanted professional images made available for events to the public through a site where people order pictures. Photographers would post pictures and people would buy them.

There are several companies that had been doing this for years. My husband's business associate felt these companies took too much in royalty fees from photographers. He wanted to create a different avenue for distributing photographers' photos and he had compiled lots of data to support his claim.

I heard about the concept and said it was a great idea but about 15 years too late. Not only had it already been done, but people now prefer instant images they take with their cell phones and can post immediately.

Fast forward, not surprisingly the owner only found data to support his idea. Then he invested time and money building out his "brainstorm of a solution." Last I checked, the photographer's mom was the only one who had purchased any images from the site.

It's vital to know how to avoid confirmation bias—important to resist the somewhat natural temptation not to factor in relevant information, thus rejecting any input that does not support your view. To overcome the pull of your own bias, you need to challenge the way you think and change the way you create solutions.

One way I personally get around this bias trap is to surround myself with people who have diverse ideas. I constantly run things by these other people, especially those who have mastered the role of playing devil's advocate.

We all know at least one person who invariably tells you why something will not work. Sometimes they are even right. It's your job to discern those times, balancing enthusiasm for a new idea with the bucket of cold water, then employing the art of choosing the right path.

Gambler's fallacy

Some entrepreneurs suffer from gambler's fallacy or reverse gambler's fallacy. Either one exists when you base future choices on past events.

A gambler's fallacy is a mistaken belief that once something happens frequently, it is less likely to continue happening. Think of tossing a coin. If you consistently throw heads, you may assume that you're due to throw tails. Except that when it comes to random odds, this fallacy is just not true.

The opposite occurs in reverse gambler's fallacy when the longer you go achieving success, the more confident you become that things will *not* change. Think of tossing that same coin. If you throw it ten times in a row and get heads each time, what are the odds it will be heads again on the eleventh throw? The odds are still 50/50 of course (unless you're using a two-headed coin), but because you got heads ten out of ten times, the odds change in your mind and you assume heads will pop up again.

In truth, odds don't change at all, but your confidence increases. Similarly, when your business is going really well and you are making lots of decisions that are working, you think you can't lose. Well, that is just plain wrong, for almost all businesses experience setbacks. Whether you prepare for setbacks or not determines if a problem will make or break you.

Several years ago, everything about my business was marked with success—revenue grew, the number of my employees increased, and we gained many additional new client projects. As a result, I thought I was really good at running a business—making decisions, hiring people, and doubling revenue.

Then I lost a big account due to an unfortunate incident with an employee. I was forced to reexamine everything I was doing and figure out how to make up for the company's shortcomings. I did learn I can handle a drop in business and come out better for it, but it took me a full year of losing $1 million in revenue to get back on track. Now I know there's no guarantee it won't happen again.

I have a client with whom I am currently working. She is smart, successful, and her business is growing like crazy. She is doing a lot of things right, but she is gambling on one area of her business based on the notion that nothing bad happened in the past. However, that does not protect her from future mistakes.

Having the courage and confidence to do things is a good trait, but not planning for a worst-case scenario leaves you exposed. It's like driving your car. You may not have had an accident in the past, but you cannot predict whether someone is going to hit you or not. Having insurance is a way of prepping and playing the odds.

Jack-of-all-trades

In psychology there is a term called "overconfidence bias." A person with this bias has too much faith in their own opinions and knowledge. He or she thinks their contribution is more valuable to a decision than it actually is.

Everyone knows someone who suffers from believing they can do everything. These people are annoying, and they impose their unrealistic decision-making on others at every opportunity.

Years ago a study was done to look into overconfidence, which is the failure to know the limits of one's knowledge. The study also looked at the illusion of control when chance, not skill, plays a part in performance. Another part of the study examined when people use a small subset of information to draw large conclusions.

Additionally, the study sought understanding of the decision to start a venture, the risk involved with the venture, and the involvement of cognitive biases in the decision-making process.

The results determined that entrepreneurs are more likely to be overconfident in their abilities as compared to the general population. Entrepreneurs tend not to see the limits of their knowledge. Plus, they perceive less risk. An illusion of control decreases their risk perception, suggesting that individuals who start ventures might not acknowledge that certain tasks important to the venture's success are beyond their control.

My husband and I have a good friend who started a distillery. We were investors and my husband was involved in the early start-up of the distillery.

I had to step back, for the founder thought he was expert in areas that he was not. While his overconfidence helped him become successful, I found it painful to be involved. For example, he had bottle labels designed with an illegible font and you could not tell what kind of liquor was in the bottle. I tried giving him feedback to improve the design—an area in which I have expertise.

He responded that his audience is more sophisticated than the average consumer and would be able to recognize his brand.

Over the years, he did change the bottle labels so they now reflect the recommendations I gave him. However, he implemented changes based on his own experience for he does not take advice or even recognize when he makes mistakes. I stopped offering advice because his overconfidence bias is great and I felt it was not worth fighting the battles.

Entrepreneurs could save themselves time and money if they would be receptive to feedback, using input from others as a safety net to keep their biases from leading them into unforeseen failure. Often a person's second or third business has a tendency to be more successful in less time, as it takes a while for entrepreneurs to admit failures and incorporate lessons learned.

Jumping off a cliff

There are many risks inherent to starting a company. Logically you would think that people who start businesses have a high risk propensity. However, research shows that is not the case. Instead, entrepreneurs don't necessarily perceive the risk involved. They assume they will learn to fly on the way down!

When a person has an illusion of control, their risk perception is minimized. For me, I was sure I would learn to manage money— a skill that is really important to the success of any business. I assumed my team and I would learn on the job. Eventually I got better at managing money, but I should have hired an expert to assist me. My company would have been more financially successful if I had obtained help early on.

Starting and running a company requires a leap of faith at one time or another. I find it's important not to let a lack of knowledge stop you from accepting challenges. Just bring in experts to help you whenever necessary.

Emotional Intelligence

The term emotional intelligence (EI) is becoming more and more prevalent. It is not just important to be smart, motivated, and ambitious. You need to show qualities of emotional intelligence too.

Emotional intelligence is the ability to understand and manage your own emotions. Plus it extends to the way you relate to your employees and other people with whom you interact. Someone with a high level of emotional intelligence is aware of their feelings and knows how their emotional reactions affect others around them.

Emotional intelligence can be learned and can improve as you grow. Daniel Goleman, an American psychologist, helped put emotional intelligence on the map and he came up with five key elements: self-awareness, self-regulation, motivation, empathy, and social skills.

1. If you're self-aware, you always know how you feel, which in turn can help you identify your strengths and weaknesses. My strength is in working with difficult situations to find resolutions. My weakness is in handling details, especially when tasks are repetitive.

2. Self-regulation is all about staying in control. One example is not letting people see you lose your temper no matter what the situation. One of my employees had anger issues that made him unpredictable. He was good at hiding these traits when we first hired him, but the longer he worked with us the more his bad behavior surfaced. Fortunately he soon quit while cursing us on the way out, saving me having to fire him.

3. Motivation helps you continually work toward goals. Highly motivated people step up and do whatever task is needed, even ones without credit or reward. They jump in and help whether a task is theirs or not. This can be the simple task of emptying the dishwasher in the company kitchen or working on a weekend to meet a deadline. These are valuable people.

4. If you have empathy, you have the ability to put yourself in someone else's situation. This is an important trait for a good leader. When I was young, I left a really good job because I received a lack of empathy. My mother was terminally ill and my boss asked when she was going to die so I would be back to work without distraction. That was an ultimate lack of empathy.

5. Entrepreneurs with good social skills are adept at managing change and resolving conflicts. When business slows

down and projects fall off, I find I am better now at managing changes that need to take place. I am also better able to predict potential conflicts arising than I was in the past. Conflicts occur but I tackle them right away, diffusing things before they get out of hand.

It's a good idea to identify areas of emotional intelligence in which you need improvement and work on them. It will help you no matter what you're doing—both professionally and personally.

Striking gold

When things go right, it is like striking gold. For me this occurs when I land a new client or project, making me feel like I am on top of the world.

Your reward may be different than mine. The key is in knowing what makes you feel successful and pursuing it. For one of my colleagues, this gold strike occurs when we hire the right employee and that person becomes integrated into the team. Then my colleague can successfully delegate some of his tasks to that individual.

I try and delegate all the things I dislike to others, for they are usually much better at those tasks than me. Thankfully I don't need to control everything. Entrepreneurs who feel they need to do everything themselves have a hard time letting go or expanding. Inevitably there comes a point when you can't do it all, so it's important to learn early on what you can successfully hand off. That will be gold to you in the future.

I have become a better leader over time. One of my past employees started her own business and told me she has a basic rule at work that involves no shouting. I thought that was funny and said I'd never done that until she reminded me I had in the early days. It was due to my inexperience and lack of self-regulation. I was super passionate about what I was doing and let it spill over when people did not live up to my expectations.

Know what makes you feel successful and pursue it.

Innovation and the future

I was lucky to hear a talk given by the Chief Innovation Officer of a large software firm. The man explained that expertise means nothing now for innovation is the future. Everything is new and people only value innovation since no one has more than five years' experience around the relatively new field of digital transformation. He said that all companies are about technology.

I listened to his lecture and tried to bring up a point about an experience I had with a large real estate company that was not adopting technology. He dismissed my point and went back to lecturing about how things had changed and the way things are now.

First of all, if your title is Chief Innovation Officer you better be pushing innovation. But after I left the talk, I found I disagreed with him on many levels. I was sitting there thinking if he ends up in the ER for medical attention, I wonder if he dismisses the physician with 20 years' expertise for the new guy who seems more innovative. Even he might bend his ways and want the person with the most experience to help him.

It's a fact that experience can help you become more innovative, especially if you discover a way to improve on a process or recognize that something is missing from a process so you can build on it. Not everyone with experience needs to become static.

A great book to read about innovation and thinking differently is *Blue Ocean Strategy*. The authors talk about creating a different way of doing things. One of my favorite examples is Cirque du Soleil, which challenged the traditional circus model and developed their own kind. Instead of building a business that caters to children, they created a business in an uncontested market space.

Cirque du Soleil's audience consists of adults and corporate clients willing to pay top dollar for unprecedented entertainment. This was truly innovative, for Cirque du Soleil reinvented the circus using their skills as entertainers to create a new market.

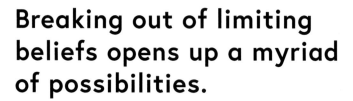

Breaking out of limiting beliefs opens up a myriad of possibilities.

CHAPTER 3:

It Takes a Team

"It's not about money. It's about the people you have, and how you're led."
—Steve Jobs, tech visionary and co-founder of Apple Inc.

"Hiring people is an art, not a science, and resumes can't tell you whether someone will fit into a company's culture. When you realize you've made a mistake, you need to cut your losses and move on."—Howard Schultz, former CEO of Starbucks

You can't do everything alone

I have been lucky to have some truly amazing hires. When you build a good team you can rely on others to support you. I find a lot of entrepreneurs want to do everything themselves and don't master the skill of delegation. These entrepreneurs become a bottleneck with the team members always waiting on something from them.

You have to let go of the idea that you are the best person to do each task. If you hire the right people they can take over. It's important to quit micromanaging.

I hear from many business owners that they want to be working *on* the business not *in* the business. But when you ask these owners how you can support them, most say they have to be the ones to do a particular task because they do it faster or better. Obviously they can't let go.

What they really love is working *in* the business since it gives them a power trip when they are the ones delivering results, closing deals, sending out proposals, and just staying in the weeds.

Relying on other people

I had the pleasure of shadowing my friend who runs a success-ful woman-owned business. I found it fun and exciting, but I also noticed there were a lot of places where she could have others doing the tasks if she would let go.

This is where the importance of good hires comes in. You have to invest in people who can support you. It's a time-consuming and sometimes painful process to teach others to do what you're used to doing, but it pays in the long run.

I have a software program I used to run for a client and I really enjoyed being involved. Now however, I have an employee who is better at running the program than I am, and he completely owns it. I still have the client relationship and work on contracts, but my employee owns all the day-to-day work. It took time to get to this place, but it was well worth it.

If you are going to build a team, use them to support you not to watch you do the work. You have to move on from being an indi-vidual contributor to an actual manager.

Being nice versus being smart

If you have a heart you are going to make this mistake. We had a fabulously loyal employee who was a delight to have around the office. She was super busy and then the work we had for her started to slow down. I continued to find things for her to do.

Eventually the work totally ran out and still I did not let her go. It took me almost six months to finally wise up and admit we no longer needed her skills in-house. I worried about office morale, but in reality, everyone knew she was coasting so my fears were unfounded.

I even worried she would have trouble finding new employment, but I had to bring my attention back to the good of the business and not of the individual. I should have been smart instead of nice, for it cost the business unnecessary money. I learned that sometimes you have to let even great employees go if you just don't have work for them to do.

Those closest to us

When you start out in business or a high-level job, one of the first things you do is think about the people you respect and want to bring onto your team. You'll be tempted to use your relationships from the past to get started. Then once you start doing well, you may make the mistake of sharing your success with those closest to you.

Having a close relationship with someone does not automatically translate into being great together in a work scenario. In fact, it often leads to the opposite. No matter who you are, you are the center of your own universe. At some point, your goals and those of others close to you will no longer converge and you'll find yourselves at odds. Rarely can you keep a personal relationship and work dynamic separate, so on unusual occasions when combining the two does work, you should value that relationship.

When it works

I have a really good friend. We started work at Microsoft the same day, meeting on the bus going to get our picture IDs taken. It was a first job for both of us. We stuck together for it was an overwhelming place to work. Plus we were two British girls working in an American company. Over the years our career paths have gone in different directions, but I can always count on her to support me.

The new owners of my company told me I was scheduled to make a presentation to one of their clients on Monday morning in California. I was informed about this Friday night. Although I had only a little information about the meeting, I knew I needed backup. I called my friend and she was delighted to go with me. I made sure to book a hotel room with fluffy towels, comfy robes, and good room service.

My friend and I worked on the presentation deck until Sunday at midnight. Wearing her cozy robe, my friend ordered room service for us and Monday morning, we presented our pitch.

There is no better feeling than being able to depend on someone who can help you get ahead. In this case, having someone close to me with whom I also have a professional relationship is amazing. She always gives me time and helps me collect my thoughts. Our ability to work well together comes from knowing and appreciating each other's skills and expertise.

My friend loved the trip. She had nothing on the line and only came to help me. And I knew what would make it appealing to her. We were home Monday night in time for dinner after having a fabulous fancy lunch on the beach—the well-worth-it price for her service.

Never hire outlaws or in-laws

Hiring the wrong employees is one of the most costly mistakes a business owner can make. You might think you'll do better than others on this score, but we all tend to make this mistake—at some point, we all hire at least one wrong person. This is particularly damaging when a business is first getting started; it can mean the difference between success and failure.

While you are likely to think you are the exception to this rule, it is human nature to feel a personal obligation to help family members when you can. After all, it makes you feel good about yourself. And as long as everything is working, it even seems like a good decision.

That is, until it's not.

In my own business, this mistake cost me more than a million dollars in lost revenue and I lost good employees too.

You might ask how I could make a million dollar mistake. Well, I started feeling good about being successful and wanted to share my success with family and friends. So I invested time and effort into family and extended family, incorrectly assuming they would be loyal and give back more in return.

I was wrong.

Beware hiring the wrong people.

Warning about family members

Since I owned my business in partnership with my husband, I already viewed my company as a family business. I erroneously thought that adding more family would not cause any issues. We did have some success in the beginning, but as the business grew, so did the family members' expectations. As their sense of entitlement grew, boundaries were crossed.

Although some families can make it work, they are rare and probably have defined roles. Making it work is the exception rather than the rule, so it's best to avoid bringing family into your business. It's much simpler.

If you need to help family and friends find employment, connect them with a good recruiter who can place them in someone else's business.

Let me share some details as a warning. I hired a skilled spouse of a close family member. At first he was a good fit, but as time elapsed, he became disgruntled. A disgruntled employee is bad enough but if he or she is related, it's a hundred times worse.

Other employees felt they could not be honest with me about this individual and his problematic behavior. His manager felt hamstrung for he didn't want to disappoint me when he couldn't make this work. Employees started to avoid working with my relative-in-law.

Eventually the problems reached me, but only when termination was looming and now I had a real problem. If I didn't terminate the problem employee, our work environment would become toxic. If I did terminate him, it would impact my family with the backlash.

In the end, mister problem-in-law walked out of the business with no notice. We lost other employees too as well as revenue—all because we thought family comes first. This was a costly mistake, including the damage it did to our family dynamics. People took sides and relationships were irreparably harmed.

If I could go back and make a change, I would never offer this particular helping hand.

Managing others

The first time I had to fire someone from my own business I was terrified. I agonized over the necessity of the decision for months.

When I finally had the courage to let the person go, a weight was lifted. I never should have doubted my intuition. I knew the person was not right for the job but I doubted my own judgment, instead putting my faith in hope. Hope did not work. Maybe I kept hoping to avoid the firing.

No firing since has been as hard. I guess the first time you do anything, there's definitely a learning curve.

Learning the hard way

I am working with a lovely client right now. It is her first business and she is doing incredibly well except for one hire she made. She has a woman employee who is holding her hostage and she is afraid to fire her.

My client first told me about this particular person two months ago and we talked about how she needed to be fired for certain actions that constituted good cause. Only a week later the woman was still employed. And now the woman was doing even more damage to the business.

I even tried to line up her replacement but my client was not ready to pull the trigger for the woman is good at one part of her job.

Fast forward two months later and we are still having the same conversation. Only now the employee is hurting the business on a daily basis. She takes time off with no notice or approval, leaving others to cover for her. She "forgets" to order key items that are fundamental to the business. Clearly she is sabotaging the company.

Yet still my client is not ready. When she finally does fire her, I know she will feel much better. But she has to arrive at the decision in her own time. Then the next person will be easier to let go.

Firing takes practice

This is a skill you need to learn. Though it is always hard to fire people, it becomes a necessity for a manager or business owner and you need to learn to do it well.

Keep in mind you are about to really mess up someone's day, so be kind. Plan all the details in advance while anticipating the questions you'll receive. Give the person privacy as well as time to collect him- or herself. No matter how hard it is for you, it is worse for the person being let go.

It is better to rip the bandage off than drag something out. I do this by giving people a little severance pay instead of keeping them on the payroll. I let them go right away and give them money to put towards whatever they need.

In the technology arena, I've witnessed some horrible reductions in workforce. We were at a big partner conference for one of the Fortune 50 companies we have as a client. The team was onstage presenting all the new offerings to the partners and talking about successes. After the keynote, the general manager received a call letting him know he was let go as the company was changing direction.

Who fires a key person at a partner conference? The general manager and his whole team got on a plane and flew home to deal with the mess; and the partners were left wondering what happened. All this showed someone clearly did not care about their employees, partners, or customers.

My business partner, Noland, is much better at firing people than I am. He prepares next steps by getting information about what that person can do for future employment. Noland is detail-oriented and that helps when you are giving bad news. At that moment, the person being fired will only focus on a worst-case scenario. My partner follows up to make sure they have what they need. It's important to be kind and let each person keep his or her dignity.

Beyond redemption

I had one firing that went horribly wrong. My employee was fudging the hours she was working for a major client. I billed the hours she reported and the client called me on it. The client was right— there was no way my employee worked 200 hours during our slowest month.

The hours did not compute and now the client wanted to drop the rate for service as the deliverables had changed.

I met with the employee and she tried to defend her hours. Then I let her know we had to drop the rate for the client. She refused to reduce her rate and we hit an impasse since now her rate was the same as the billing rate, leaving no money for overhead or company profit.

I told her we were going to have to part ways. She got really angry and stomped out. On her way out the door, I reminded her that the contract was with our company and not with her.

The next day I got to the client site and my former employee was sitting outside the client's door. I had already fired her but there she was ostensibly working. I asked what she was doing there and she started screaming I was harassing her.

She was totally combative and people started coming out of their offices. My only option was to call security and have her removed. Fortunately, my client stepped in and told her to calm down. He asked me to step away so he could talk to her. He told her she was making a scene and she was no longer welcome there. She finally left.

Don't forget the client knew she was fabricating her hours and I had told him I was going to let her go as I could not support that behavior.

Long story short, she got hired full-time by the client in another department. It is a better fit for her since she has to be there physically every day. She just wants to be paid for being present and she can now literally bill hours for just showing up.

To this day she will not speak to me and is convinced I was wrong to let her go. It is weird at times, but I just take the high road. I stepped in to her work and then replaced her with someone much better. Between my client and me, all is forgotten.

You can't do everything alone. You certainly can't run a business alone, not if you want to scale it, not if you want it to grow.

CHAPTER 4:

Inevitable Mistakes

"Even a mistake may turn out to be the one thing necessary to a worthwhile achievement."— Henry Ford, industrialist and business magnate

"The biggest mistake was that I didn't hire all the right people. I should have done better reference checks. I should have defined the roles in a much more professional manner. I hired people who just couldn't do the job."
— Lillian Vernon, founder and CEO of catalog business

Mistakes—we all make them, whether we're business owners, executives or employees.

If we're not making them, we're not doing enough.

The trick is learning from our inevitable missteps, then recovering and eventually prospering afterward.

So how to do this…

Experience counts

I don't think you really recognize your strongest abilities until a project is over. That's why you get better in your second and third businesses, which is one of the many reasons to do more than one thing during your career.

After you've done something once, you don't take as long debating a course of action. At that point, you have experience behind you and are less likely to agonize and more likely to take quicker action.

I've learned to recognize patterns in my own management style as well as in the people around me. I've also learned to trust my intuition.

Pivotal moments

If I knew more about money when I started my professional career, I'd certainly have a lot more of it now. I made a lot of mistakes and took some risks that did not pay off.

However, I feel pretty confident that I will land on my feet and I certainly have an entertaining ride. I was just talking with my Dad and he said he tells everyone his daughter has her ups and downs but never sits around with her head in the sand when things go wrong. I take that as the ultimate compliment.

It is a trait of successful people that you can't dwell on your mistakes as there will be many. The first time I lost money I thought, "Wow! I finally have something to lose."

My biggest mistake

At first, I never paid much attention to money. I thought if I had money coming in, I was doing great. I never knew to look at what money was actually going out the door. So the more I made, the more I spent. To top it off, I invested in the wrong people, putting energy into people with issues rather than rock stars in their areas of expertise. I learned the hard way. But then isn't that the truth with most of us?

I learned over time it's not how much money you make, it's how much money you keep that really matters. When my top line was great, I tended to get lazy and pay less attention to my business. When business was tight, I pulled things in out of necessity.

So I really only learned how to run a business once I started to lose money.

Leaving money on the table

When I was an employee, I left money on the table by not taking the full match for my 401K. Now as a business owner, I love it when people don't take the full match. I can discern someone's money habits merely by looking at their 401K choices and pay-checks. I can tell who is an ant and who is a grasshopper.

One version of the fable titled *The Ant & the Grasshopper* describes how the ant works hard and saves everything whereas the grasshopper spends his time living in the moment and having fun. When winter comes, the grasshopper has to beg for food from the ant and is refused.

I advise people to increase their 401K contribution when they get a raise. I have one employee who took two years off and traveled the world. He came back to work for us after having an amazing time living off his savings plus the income he earned from renting his house. He worked it out so he never tapped into his 401K.

I have had other employees who were let go and panicked. They had nothing saved for they were out trying the best restaurants and having a good time without thinking ahead for the long term.

It is said by some that it is great to be the child of an ant—your parents spend their lives planning for your future and what they can leave behind for you. On the other hand, children of grass-hoppers need to have their own savings plans!

The bad news for ants is that they have a hard time spending money. They don't know when they should actually tap into their own investments. Instead they are always squirreling away for a rainy day. Whereas the merit of grasshoppers is that they tend to take on more risk, which can potentially lead to greater profit.

I think of myself as a grasshopper with a savings plan—sort of a cross between the two.

It's how much money you keep that really matters.

Doing everything yourself

Entrepreneurs and others who are top performers often think they can do everything better than anyone else. And they think it is quicker to just do something themselves rather than asking others to do it. After all, it is almost too painful to train people for it takes time.

Avoid this trap as it will be your downfall. The art of delegation is what will enable you to grow and scale.

Of course, to do this effectively, you need the right people to whom you can delegate.

Building your team will take time and experience. You are not going to get an A-team right out of the starting gate. Even if you are lucky enough to do so in the beginning, you might not be able to keep them. Therefore it's important to learn how to teach others and allow them to have the authority that goes hand-in-hand with responsibility.

In consulting for one of my clients' businesses, I obtained feedback from her employees on what they liked and disliked about the company. One of the complaints was that the boss wanted to do everything, including that person's job. The boss seemed to think the employee's job more fun than her own.

The employee needed to make more money, and without the satisfaction from work she wasn't getting to do, she was seriously considering looking for another job. The boss was oblivious to the fact she was taking over someone else's role—stepping on the toes of an employee. Fortunately, in time the boss figured it out and went back to her own job. Everyone was happy.

Allow people to do what you hire them to do. If they make mistakes, which is inevitable for we all make mistakes, create teachable moments and show them to handle things differently.

Meanwhile, consult a therapist if you need help curbing your perfectionist tendencies. This personality trait may serve you well as an individual contributor, but it's a roadblock in building a team.

Being able to let things go when they are not perfect but are good enough, is hard. But it's worth it; for in the long run, delegation will help your business expand.

Imagine if one of your team members is actually able to do something better than you can do it yourself. When this happens, and it likely will, don't feel threatened. Feel empowered instead and move on to another task.

Overcoming obstacles

At one time, I was the biggest obstacle standing in my own way. As with many entrepreneurs, my desire to be in control would take over.

Just last night I heard a business owner say, "When I don't manage everything myself, things go wrong. I have to do everything myself or it is not done right." That sentence should ring a bell with some of you.

I was having dinner with some friends one Sunday night when I watched a friend take a phone call. Someone on her team was canceling an event due to an unforeseen conflict.

My friend's instinct was to avoid disappointing everyone involved by stepping in to cover for her employee. That would have been a great tactic, but my friend doesn't have the skills to take over the other person's role. I suggested it was better to cancel the event rather than try to cover with the wrong skill set.

You may think you should step into such a scenario, but it may cause more damage than it does good. In this case, the event will be much better with the original qualified person delivering it. Though participants will be temporarily disappointed due to the delay, they will appreciate the event once they experience it the optimum way.

Covering for someone when you are without the appropriate skills, even to avoid disappointing people, will lead to a negative situation.

My friend ignored my advice. She was so worried what the other participants would think that she made the decision to go ahead and cover it anyway, despite her lack of qualifications for the project. I was frustrated watching the whole thing unfold. Needless to say, it did not go well.

Room in the kitchen

I have three wonderful aunts and they are all good cooks. When everyone gets together you can imagine the dynamic—lots of feathers get ruffled and feelings get hurt. It's like watching a horse race waiting to see who is going to win. Everyone else has learned to stay out of the kitchen and out of the way.

The first time one of my aunts came to visit me, I cooked dinner and she was amazed I can cook. I laughed since she did not know I have any culinary skills as there is never room for me in the kitchen at a family event.

The point is that sometimes people will pleasantly surprise you. Other times they may let you down. However, if you don't make room for others to try, you'll be the only one in the kitchen wondering why everyone else is enjoying the results of your labor while you're still standing at the stove.

Boosting profitability

I never focused on profitability when I first started my business. I thought if I was making money, it was a good thing. But making money is not the same as being profitable.

When you first start out in business, you will likely need to take on what is called portfolio work. Everyone you pitch will want to see what you have done for other customers. Landing that first project is the hardest and in most cases it will actually cost you money. But you must do it to have a sample you can share.

A good way to land one of these first customers is to pitch a nonprofit. They can't afford high rates, but they are willing to work with you to get the work done. They make excellent clients of first projects. You get the practice and they get the results.

There used to be a rule of thumb that you should break your business into three parts. The first third was the cost of paying your employees. Second was paying for the cost of running the business. Third was profit.

I have found that in reality profits are much less. If you earn a profit of 30 percent, you are doing amazingly well, 20 percent and you are doing great, 15 percent and you are doing well. If your profits are only 10 percent or less, you need to cut costs and adjust prices upward.

In my company, our employees cost 60 percent, the cost of running the business is about 20 percent, and we are in good shape if we have a 20 percent profit. But our goal was to be at 30 percent profit. Using a blend of projects that had higher margins mixed with some that were much less, it took us awhile to master the mix.

The point is to know when a project is profitable. And it's absolutely necessary to get rid of a client if they are costing you money unless you have a strong strategic reason for keeping them. It is fine to take on work that you know will cost the business money if it helps land future work.

Don't undervalue yourself

If you shop at discounts stores, you get discount customers. If you want a higher-end clientele, you need to believe in your ability and charge accordingly.

Right after I sold my company, I was asked to do some consulting. Since I was no longer carrying overhead, I offered to lower my regular rate without even being asked. What I didn't anticipate was that I would be treated with less respect than I received when I was billing at the higher rate.

I would never have cut my price when bidding for a project with my team in mind. When setting a price for just my own time, I treated the situation differently—and that was my mistake. I won't make this mistake again.

Impostor syndrome

In psychology, the "impostor syndrome" is when an individual has a fear or feeling of being found out as fake with no credentials. It is the feeling that, regardless of your accomplishments, you're still about to be unmasked as a fraud.

The term dates back to 1978 when two psychologists, writing in *Psychotherapy: Theory, Research, and Practice,* identified the impostor phenomenon in high-achieving women. Many people suffer from it but it's definitely more prevalent among women than men.

It's a form of waiting for another shoe to drop. Even individuals who reach success with something like a hit song or bestselling novel often fear they can't duplicate their success.

The more professional skills and education many women acquire, the less confident they may feel. This can contribute to their suffering from impostor syndrome.

If you feel like you don't belong, are not a great leader, or just don't know enough—be assured you are not alone.

How to fix it

If you want others to value what you do, you first have to believe in yourself. Too often we're surrounded by naysayers and this contributes to our distress.

Instead, find a positive cheerleader—not someone who misleads you, but a person who tells you the truth when you're good or even great at what you do.

A few well-placed words will frequently make all the difference in your attitude. Astute customers and employees will note your positive attitude and reflect positive energy back to you.

It's not how many times you fall down; it's how many times you get up. Just remember: you can't and won't win them all.

CHAPTER 5:

Those You Trust (including yourself)

"The best executive is the one who has sense enough to pick good men to do what he wants done, and self-restraint to keep from meddling with them while they do it."—Theodore Roosevelt, 26th President of the United States

This goes for women too!

"Hire people who are better than you are, then leave them to get on with it. Look for people who will aim for the remarkable, who will not settle for the routine."—David Ogilvy, advertising tycoon

A valuable commodity

Trust is the most valuable characteristic you can ask of others. It allows you to count on them, rely on them, and believe they've got your back as well as the best interests of your company.

Obviously, no one is going to care about your business as much as you do. But knowing that others will not sabotage or hinder your progress, and instead will foster it, is vital to the success of your organization.

Enjoy it. Savor it. Revel in it for it's rare. It's a combination of choosing the right people and interacting with them in a positive, forthright and encouraging manner—a combination that works beautifully when all the stars are aligned.

Setting and achieving goals

School didn't come easily to me so I learned to try harder. I was always determined, as evidenced by my earning a Ph.D. despite difficulties.

I never expect things to go my way in business either, so I start companies and projects anticipating that I will need to work harder than everyone else to succeed.

Those who always expect grades and contracts to go their way, tend not to have tools for overcoming adversity when the inevitable happens and something in their plans goes astray.

After all, it's not how hard you're knocked down, for that happens to everyone eventually. Instead it's how quickly and determinedly you get back up and keep going. It's about how adept you are at conquering or overcoming obstacles that bodes well for your ultimate success.

Free advice is useless

Many of us rarely take advice from people when it is free, but we pay careful attention if we spend money for that same advice.

We hear valuable things all the time but often dismiss them as trivial because they don't come from "an expert."

Joshua Bell is one of the best concert violinists in the world. He played for free, for 45 minutes, on a violin worth $3.5 million at a Metro subway station in Washington, D.C. Just seven people stopped to hear him play and one was a 3-year-old boy whose parent soon hurried him along. Only one person recognized Bell in the rush hour crowd that was coming and going on the subway.

Significantly, tickets for one of Bell's shows generally cost hundreds of dollars. His perceived value is obviously much greater if you've paid for a ticket and you're listening in a venue you believe is worthwhile. Granted the people in the subway were busy and in a hurry to get to work, but his music was just as precious as if in a concert.

The takeaway is to invest something—whether time or money—into something so you perceive it as valuable. This matters most if you want to learn about something. Given human nature, it has to cost something for you to pay attention.

Short- and long-term gratification

I have a number in my head that I need in my nest egg in order to stop working. It is a number I determined on my own, based on very little but it is *mine* and I'm committed to it. It represents my comfort level.

I have been working with a relative on how to set goals and get ahead in life. He is the most lovable guy around—helpful, kind, energetic, polite and fun. However, he is a terrible decision maker. If a sign says, "Don't touch this as you will die a horrible painful death," he would touch it to see if it was true.

When everyone is running from a burning building, he would be the guy going in. He would have made a wonderful Marine or firefighter. In fact, if someone said I can take one person to a desert island with me, I'd pick him for he would be perfect.

One of my relative's traits is he always over-complicates everything. If you ask him a question, he gets into some far-fetched theory. Included with his answer are his hopes and dreams—overly complicated.

I finally gave him two rules to follow:

The first is to set a financial goal. Let's say it is to have $50,000 in savings to buy a house.

The second goal is to ask himself if the thing you are about to do gets you one step closer to achieving the first goal. If it does not, don't do it. If the answer is yes, then do it.

However, if there is a justifiable reason why he wants to spend money on something outside the goal, he should do that too.

He can still have dreams, but having dreams without a plan ensures they remain just dreams.

Confidence and finding your tribe

The funny thing about confidence is that we all lack it at some point in our careers. We second-guess our choices or think our skills are not good enough. We compare ourselves to women like the founder of Spanx, Sara Blakely, who is one of the first self-made women billionaires of the world. By comparing ourselves to such rarified superstars, we think we are failures and don't measure up.

To be successful, you need to surround yourself with people who challenge you to do more. Being motivated is more than half the battle.

I found my tribe in other successful entrepreneurs. Whether they moved up the corporate ladder (which is really, really hard to do), started their own businesses, or figured out ways to solve problems, I love women and men who take risks–those who start something and try different things to get ahead.

I am always drawn to people who are creative and don't let obstacles stand in their way. Lots of people say, "I could have done that." But it's the ones who actually do those things who impress me.

I heard a talk about controlling emotions in a healthy way and it really resonated with me. The point is that if you're alive, you're going to experience feeling unwanted and you're going to be stressed at times too. The only time this isn't true is once you're dead.

It's impossible to have a meaningful career without some stress and discomfort–it's part of the contract. Of course you should manage and minimize negative feelings, but trying to avoid feeling disappointed altogether won't get you anywhere. A loss of confidence *will* happen–it happens to all of us–but if you keep going and tell yourself to find a way, your belief in yourself will come back.

Managerial blinders

Just because something worked in the past does not mean it will work in the future. One of my favorite books is *Willful Blindness* by Margaret Heffernan. She teaches that we can challenge our biases when we confront facts and fears. She says we find excuses and create alternative interpretations to protect ourselves with our illusions. We do this in both our personal and our professional lives.

How can we learn not to wear blinders? There are some simple, but difficult, things you can do. First, don't be afraid of change. Second, don't shy away from conflict; though conflict is uncomfortable, it's important to learn to be okay while being uncomfortable.

You can't focus on details and also be the person visualizing the big picture. Instead you need a team to support you.

Resist the urge to immediately know the right answer instead of going through the process of examining options.

Also resist the urge to be a pleaser. We tend to make fun of people who do their own thing and are not afraid to be different.

However, these are the free thinkers who come up with the best out-of-the-box ideas.

The carrot and the old goat

I love animals. For a long while I volunteered at an animal sanctuary every other Saturday. The work made me feel wonderful for giving back. That is until one day my momentum was killed by a twenty-something supervisor without a lot of sensitivity.

For background, I always stopped by a couple of supermarkets on my way to the sanctuary to pick up old produce for the animals to give them as treats. I figured out which animals liked what and used it as my secret weapon to make friends with the animals.

From volunteering at the sanctuary, I learned two valuable lessons. One was that I wanted, even craved, recognition. I would show up in the wintertime and sometimes I was the only one on a shift. I would feel down until one day I realized I wanted someone to recognize my contribution and say "great job."

After I figured out the animals loved seeing me if I brought them bananas, strawberries and other treats, I understood I needed to do the job for them, not for recognition. That day I started working there for the right reason and it made me feel good. That is, until one day it didn't.

This leads me to the second lesson, which caused me to stop volunteering there. That was the day the twenty-something supervisor told me I might have killed a goat. The goat died on one of the days I was volunteering and he died by choking on a carrot. Since I was known to feed the animals, I became the prime suspect.

When she accused me, the supervisor did say she knew I probably didn't do it on purpose. That was when I arrived for my Saturday shift two weeks later. Big signs were posted all over the barns saying, "Do not feed the animals."

The truth was the goat was elderly and had trouble swallowing. He had somehow gotten a carrot, choked and died. I don't know much about goats, but I do believe they will eat just about anything. People even hire goats to clear a field of brambles as a green alternative to clearing the brush.

In my defense, I never fed the goat a carrot and if I had, I would have tried a Heimlich maneuver on old Billy (real name changed to protect his identity).

Don't get me wrong, I was distraught. I retraced my steps in my mind, remembering what fruit and vegetables I fed each animal. The goats and sheep had a thing for bananas and went crazy for them. The pigs liked watermelons and strawberries. The llamas loved things that tasted sweet. One donkey and a horse were on a restricted diet and could only have lettuce. And the blind pony loved carrots.

In other words, I knew what every animal could and couldn't have. No one had ever said, "Don't feed carrots to the goats." Nor did it ever come up that Billy had a hard time swallowing. It was just an accident and poor Billy was on his last legs from a hard life.

But even though I knew I wasn't responsible, being blamed for the incident caused me to quit. The girl had accused me and could not take that back. Plus what I loved about my volunteer job changed that day, for what had brought me joy—bringing pleasure to the animals—was now gone.

An inexperienced supervisor misspoke and as a consequence, the sanctuary lost my services as a regular volunteer.

The big takeaway is not to give under-qualified people too much power. They can kill your employee momentum and enthusiasm. You may lose good people for reasons you will never hear about.

The director of the sanctuary was bummed I quit. And even though I didn't kill the goat, he's never far from my thoughts. I still miss Billy the Goat.

Valuable lessons often show up in odd places.

Giving power to the wrong people can have disastrous effects.

CHAPTER 6:

Money Matters

"Money is only a tool. It will take you wherever you wish, but it will not replace you as the driver." –Ayn Rand, novelist and philosopher

Lessons from the Middle East

My father always tells me, "If you never ask, you're never going to get it."

Dad went from being a communications specialist to becoming a defense contractor working in the Middle East. There he was working in a region where no price tags are put on anything, even vegetables. In the markets, the chickens are live and you have to ask the vendors to kill, pluck and prepare the chickens. I'll never forget the look on Dad's face when he realized that he failed to negotiate for a plucked dead chicken.

In lieu of price tags, everything in the Mideast is a negotiation. And for foreigners, everything is priced differently than it is for the locals.

By dealing with the same people all the time, you learn who you can trust. And you realize it's important to consistently work with people you trust.

Early on I found out it's an advantage that I'm not afraid of money or of talking about it. When people are asked, "How much money will this project cost?" they are often afraid to bid the right price for fear of losing the business. Yet if their bid is not enough for the amount of work involved, they are equally afraid of losing out on a fair payment.

Like in the Middle East where negotiation is a way of life, it's vital to always have the skill of asking for what you need. All the other party can say is "no." In business, you can't fear that word.

The art of negotiation

No matter what role you play in an organization, you will inevitably end up having to deal with money. As the owner of a company, this is even more so. And money is something that scares people.

This is true whether you are a first-time consultant setting an hourly rate or the owner of a company setting a budget while looking for a reliable supplier. The money aspect of the process almost always triggers fear. After all, who among us knows how to best handle budget negotiations?

Although I am not afraid of money or of discussing it, I still get nervous every time I submit a proposal. I'm usually afraid I did not ask for enough and my estimate will be off. I certainly don't want to be guilty of leaving money on the table. I've come to understand that this reaction of mine is normal.

To compensate for the natural propensity to doubt ourselves, I do my best to find out about the budget before submitting a proposal. To do this, I simply ask. Nine times out of ten, the person I ask will share budget numbers with me. If the person doesn't share, it's either because he or she is new to handling budgets or may want to get something cheaply from me.

If you have gone through a home or apartment remodel, you will be able to relate to getting a bid on the cost of a project. The contractor may tell you a new kitchen will cost $50,000 and you agree to proceed. Then at the end of the project, you are handed a bill for $75,000. You feel cheated and want to know why the bill is so much higher than the quote.

Remember this scenario whenever you have to bid on a project. It's better to bid high and actually come in a little under bid rather than coming in over budget. Coming in over budget really annoys people, causing them to lose trust quickly.

An astute principle to remember: It's often best to under promise and over deliver.

And don't hesitate to ask about the amount in the budget as well as detailed questions about whatever you need to know to understand the nature of the problem. The more questions you ask, the more information you'll obtain to ensure an accurate estimate. If you're hiring someone, answer their questions too.

Pursuing wrong-sized projects

If I think a project will cost $150,000 to complete, I know to factor in three rounds of review. If the client only has $10,000 in their budget, there's no point in our talking.

Therefore it's important to know what range is involved to see if the deal is even feasible.

Many companies bid on projects that aren't right for them. Don't try to be a jack-of-all-trades for you will end up not doing anything well. Instead become known for being the best at something. This rule applies to all jobs and all roles.

And if you have a guiding principle, stick to it. For example, I always try to deliver the best customer service to my clients. I go out of my way to make things easy for them. I am known for this.

When negotiating, don't be afraid to ask how much money is involved. It's vital to find out upfront. This goes for hiring too.

There's no sense offering $100,000 to a prospect if he or she is expecting $200,000.

Estimating is a science

After I know a client's budget, I estimate the time a task will take, multiplying the number of hours by the appropriate hourly rate. I add in at least a 25 percent buffer since most of the time we all underestimate how long things will actually take.

If you're working with technical people, you should consider using a 50 percent buffer since they almost always think projects will go faster than is reasonably accurate. This is something I learned the hard way.

Once I calculate the hours for each task or role, I come up with a total. If my estimate is greater than the budget, I look for features or items to eliminate. If my estimate is much less than the budget, I know I missed something important so I go back and reevaluate.

Obviously, not everyone will share their budget even after you ask. In such cases, I build in a range to my bid. I always like to add in wiggle room so I don't have to come back to the customer and ask for more money. That is, unless the project changes significantly. If this happens, you need to address the changes immediately. Be brave and let the client know the changes will cost more money.

Think back to your kitchen remodel. No contractor ever put in a better cabinet than the one you paid for just because it looked better or had a soft close. You had to pay for it if you wanted upgrades.

So why would you ever consider giving away extras just because the customer changes his or her project scope? Just because confronting the issue of money makes you uncomfortable? You shouldn't let a little discomfort stop you. Instead, prepare yourself to have a conversation with the customer to let him or her know there will be extra costs. It may be a bit difficult, but it's abso-lutely necessary.

During this conversation, make sure you get agreement on the changes and associated costs. I've lost a lot of money not obtain-ing agreement on change requests when they first take place. I've learned my lesson and you can learn from my mistake.

My brother is a plastic surgeon. He always gets payment upfront for surgeries and procedures not covered by insurance. He says it's hard to get back a tummy tuck once the patient doesn't pay and walks out the door—a good lesson for each of us in every profession.

Knowing your worth

In business we don't always remember our value. I have a close friend who has incredible organizational skills. She can take a room that has been hit by a virtual or literal hurricane and orga-nize the hell out of it—complete with sticky labels and a calmness you never knew existed. She won't stop until the task is complete and she won't take a penny for doing it.

That's all great until you get to the last sentence, for people take advantage of her all the time. Other people recognize her worth and exploit it. My friend, we'll call her Anne, thinks everyone can do what she does, and she thinks she's just helping out.

Anne is always happy to help at first until she finds herself stuck doing things for someone she'd rather not help. Favors for friends can end up being full-time jobs that cross all sorts of boundaries.

If this sounds familiar, don't minimize your skills in your own mind. Whether you're an expert at organization, accounting, painting, designing, flower arranging, baking, managing employees or projects—take time to acknowledge your self-worth. Except for the narcissists among us who are busy vying to be the center of attention, we all need to remind ourselves of our value on a regular basis.

Borrowing money

If you own or run a business, there is a chicken and egg problem called money—it takes money to grow a company and yet it often requires growth to make that money. As a result of this conundrum, you need to find ways to obtain necessary money, perhaps by increasing the number of your customers. Of course, this is easier said than done.

Other options include borrowing money and seeking investors. Obviously, you need to be creative with money.

I started my business by taking out a line of credit on my house, the same kind of loan you would use to remodel. Instead I used the funds to cover payroll, cash flow, and large purchases. I did this since I had not yet established business credit and it was simply the easiest route to take. Having a little equity in my house gave me the confidence to take chances with the business. As a result, I didn't lose sleep when an invoice was late getting paid by one of my customers.

While there were risks using my home as collateral for my business, there were also a few perks that seemed to outweigh the risks. For one, I could charge the company interest on whatever money I loaned the business, just as a bank would. The business would pay me back with interest. This was awesome as I made up to a 15 percent return on my money, setting up a loan repayment plan with myself.

If you follow suit, you need to look up all the rules on interest rates and work with your CPA, but this method worked for me. The other plus to this arrangement was my ongoing knowledge that I had funds to cover unexpected expenses.

In my multimillion-dollar business, I usually averaged owing myself $100,000. I paid down the loan when cash flow was good and used it when cash flow was weak. Not until our fourth year in business were we able to secure a line of credit based on our business accounts receivable rather than on our personal property

With this in mind, set realistic expectations about borrowing money. If you have good personal credit, you should have an easier time getting a working line of credit established.

There are always risks involved in borrowing money, so carefully analyze your needs first.

If only

If only it were possible for me to get a do-over, a mulligan (golf term for second chance), I would hire a part-time chief financial officer (CFO) for my first business. We didn't need anyone full-time, but having a financial strategy early on would have made a huge difference. Creating a financial strategy on my own turned out to be my biggest weakness.

It's certainly true that the smartest executives hire people around them with skills that augment and supplement their own. I learned too late that I could have found a mentor through the Small Business Administration (SBA) and its resource partner SCORE, which provides expert business mentors on a volunteer basis.

I could have found someone who was a CFO in a previous time of life and who just wanted to work part-time. Unfortunately, I never filled this important role and it cost me a lot of money in lost revenue and opportunity.

If you're unable to hire a CFO for some reason, make sure you have a stellar bookkeeper and CPA firm. Use the bookkeeper to keep track of daily expenses, accounts receivable and payable, etc. Have the CPA firm set up your books so expenses are tracked to show profit and loss on a monthly basis.

Gold bars not gold stars

We all like recognition and hopefully we're motivated by more than just a paycheck and stock options. Still, this is business and the bottom line is how much money we make.

Awards and titles are lovely and they help advance careers. But again, the point of why we're working is that we're dependent upon sales translating to profits translating to wealth.

If you're not increasing your income, you should rethink what you're doing.

After all, the necessity of paying for things does not go away. Bills keep coming and the needs for material things like food and transportation and shelter don't change.

What may need to change is the strength of your determination to get ahead.

"Real" costs

Do you know your cost of goods? That was a foreign concept to me in the beginning. I didn't go to business school and didn't know it's important to know all your numbers.

Now I watch every episode of *Shark Tank* and *The Profit*, cringing when budding entrepreneurs do not know their numbers. Like how much does something cost to manufacture? What is the sales price of the item? What about your profit margin? These are all things you need to know.

If you're starting a service business, it's vital to know your employee costs; these included salary, health insurance, taxes, and a 401k match if you offer it. Everyone needs to know their employee cost number. For instance, I know that for every dollar I pay someone in my field, it costs me 35 percent above his or her salary to cover my cost of doing business. My overhead includes paying for office space, the bookkeeper, the creative director, utilities, taxes, and benefits.

Inflated views

I hire a lot of consultants whose expectations are out of whack. Some are former employees of corporations that hire consultants; these individuals tend to think everyone gets paid really high rates. These consultants fail to take into consideration the cost of a company doing business.

After all, if an agency charges $150 an hour for a consultant, most likely the consultant is getting paid less than half that rate.

Other individuals requesting high rates are those who previously commanded top dollar. However these former high earners generally fail to recognize changes in the landscape that arise from competition with outsourced suppliers, which causes rates to come down. Companies no longer have to pay as much since there are many willing to work for less.

"You drive a hard bargain"

I've heard this more than once and view it as quite the compliment. After all, I can either earn someone's love or respect. In business, I'll strive for respect every time.

If I can't properly represent myself, how can my customers count on me to handle their issues?

Anything is possible, especially when you visualize the outcome. Make sure to envision financial success for yourself and your business.

CHAPTER 7:

Marketing and Self-Promotion

"Find your voice, shout it from the rooftops, and keep doing it until the people that are looking for you find you."—Dan Harmon, writer, producer, and actor

"We are what we repeatedly do. Excellence, then, is not an act, but a habit."— often attributed to Aristotle, ancient Greek philosopher

Creating a story for your brand

I have a confession to make. I ran a marketing/communications company and we created a brand, but we never had a great story. We took on work that our clients wanted done and it helped us become successful. But when we went to pitch new work, we did not have a cohesive brand.

We became known as the company that did a little bit of everything. What we did consistently that really helped was our excellent customer service and ability to execute.

A company that has a clear brand does better. My friend who owns a distillery has a clear brand. He created a story first and built on that story to sell his product. I laugh when I hear the story for some of it is fictional and some of it is truth, but that does not matter. He sells the story and his customers love it. In fact, he believes his own story now. He does not stray from that story to make additional money through tangential products. He creates liquor and sells liquor, living and breathing his brand.

Staying current

I was lucky to be accepted into a "Women in Cloud" program sponsored by Microsoft and Hewlett Packard Enterprise (HPE), and run by Meylah Corporation. The program is geared to help women who run technology firms accelerate their growth. Fewer than two percent of all women who run companies are in the technology sector.

What this program does is focus on ways to develop strategies for building recurring revenue. In other words, it's great to develop a solution you can sell over and over. The program is also built to help unblock some of the issues business owners experience. It provides mentorship, support, and access to funding.

Since I am passionate about women in technological careers, I am excited about being involved with this program. And it certainly never hurts to learn more about recurring revenue tactics. After all, that's the best way to accrue wealth.

And I totally believe in education, as you'll see from my personal story.

Move to America

I moved to the United States when I was about to go to college; I've since become a dual citizen. I came to the American university system with no SAT scores. At first I went to community college; then once I adapted, I transferred to Towson University in Maryland. There I earned joint bachelor's and master's degrees in psychology.

It turns out I like data and I also like working with animals. I'm no good at being a counselor because I want to tell people what to do instead of letting them work it out for themselves.

What I really enjoy is discovering people's business needs and coming up with solutions that can be implemented. I also like developing schedules, managing deliverables, and creating things out of virtually nothing.

From lost rat to working with data

In graduate school I took an internship at the NIH Gerontology Research Center. I had the job of what was technically called a "rat runner" in a laboratory studying aging.

The rats run through a maze and in order to handle each rat, you pick it up by its tail and swing it so it can't bite you. On day one, I swung a rat and then let go, after which the rat got lost in the ventilation system. My boss decided right away that rat running is not my thing. So he gave me work entering data instead.

It turns out I'm really good at graphs and visual images. In my new role, I spent hours creating graphs for all sorts of publications. This was at a time when creating a graph was a difficult process of trial and error.

My boss discovered I'm also good with people. So he had me meet families of newly visiting scientists and help them get settled into the community. I sorted out their basic needs as they struggled to figure how things work here in what was to them a foreign country.

Having lived abroad, I knew the difficulty of figuring out the basics—things that most of us take for granted like going to a grocery store all the way to figuring out how to get kids enrolled in school or finding a place to live. I liked helping the scientists and their families.

Make time for yourself away from working in the rat race.

More education

In graduate school I taught an undergraduate psychology class and became an adjunct professor when I was just 22 years old.

I decided to enter a Ph.D. program to study Ergonomics and Human Factors. The simplest way to describe my field is it's a study of the way people interact with things around them. Human Factors is also known as functional design; it is the practice of designing products, systems, or processes to take into account the interaction between them and the people who use them.

At the time, human computer interaction (HCI) was a new area with a lot of research being done. I'm not a good test taker in the American system but I'm really good at the work. Thus I had to be creative about how I got accepted into the program.

Catholic University in Washington, D.C., took me as a Ph.D. candidate on a provisional basis. I really wanted to do this program and was told I needed all A's and B's otherwise I would be dropped.

Dr. Marc Sebrechts was my advocate and supporter, and he made this possible.

I got a teaching assistant position to pay half my tuition and worked as a bartender to pay the rest.

I was able to enter the Ph.D. program by completely selling myself. I passed all my classes in graduate school with a 3.9 average (out of 4.0). Earning my Ph.D. is by far one of my greatest accomplishments.

I'm good at getting money and talking people into things too. It's all a matter of how you market yourself and your requests. While at Catholic University, I had an internship with the Army Research Institute. Through them I landed a large grant for the university on virtual reality (VR). My mentor, Dr. Joseph Psotka, was incredibly innovative and he paid for the VR lab equipment. His influence was key in my pursuing a career in technology.

The technologies I studied 25 years ago have become standard today. Artificial intelligence and virtual reality are now on the front edge.

Investing in marketing

The other day I was introduced to a business owner who runs two restaurants. She asked me what types of marketing efforts she should engage in to increase her sales.

The first question I asked is, "Who are your customers? Are they locals, tourists or a mix?" This makes a huge difference for it's vital to know first and foremost who it is that your business is targeting and serving. Then the next question is, "Who do you want to attract?"

Since her restaurants cater to the local community and not the tourist industry, she needs customers year-round. I suggested she start a loyalty program that gives regular customers a discount. She will benefit by learning about their habits and the customers will feel appreciated.

Whether you are running a restaurant, spa or any other type of business, people need to know about you. And they need to know what services or products you offer. Thus you need to invest in ways to increase your visibility. If you have enough customers but want to tell them about new offerings, marketing can certainly help. If you want the business to show up as a top search result, marketing is necessary.

A mistake most businesses make is in not knowing their audience or their market share. It's necessary to know who will buy or use a company's services and products. Guessing isn't good enough; even assumptions based on experience are insufficient. After all, the truth may differ in real ways from your guesswork.

Once you've identified and understand your users, you can promote directly to their needs. Keep in mind that people don't always know what they need. It is your job to help them understand how you can help them solve a problem.

The big takeaway: You can have the best business idea in the world, but if no one knows about it, you won't be successful.

Making it big

Look at Starbucks Coffee. They did all the market research, figuring out where they should place their stores. A competitor—Tully's Coffee—just put their stores opposite the Starbucks. Tully's built a business using Starbucks' successful footprint and standing in its shadow.

In 1992, Tom "Tully" O'Keefe was a Seattle-based real estate developer who understood Starbucks had no competitors since he was leasing space to Starbucks on a regular basis. Six months later, O'Keefe took this knowledge and his lifelong love of coffee, and founded Tully's.

Tully's focused on growing the brand rather than seeking profits. In 2000 alone, Tully's opened 50 stores, helping to make them a real competitor to Starbucks. Then a string of bad luck and bad timing changed things.

Later analysis showed Tully's employed too many people to turn a profit compared to their competitors—Starbucks, Caribou, and Peet's Coffee. Plus Tully's failed to stop trying to look and act like Starbucks. Everyone knows about Starbucks but much fewer remember Tully's. Marketing the way Starbucks does it certainly works.

Another example is Jenny Craig versus Nutrisystem. Both are weight loss, weight management, and nutrition companies.

Jenny Craig was founded in Australia in 1983 and Nutrisystem was founded in the United States in 1972. For awhile in the 1990s, if you saw a Nutrisystem store, Jenny Craig was right around the same corner. They were definitely targeting the same audience and both were using celebrity spokespersons.

Nutrisystem changed their business model, getting rid of their brick and mortar stores and moving to a direct to consumer food delivery and online service. Jenny Craig still has weight loss centers. Both businesses diversified their approach and both found their niche.

Turkey farming in the UK

My cousin John came to visit us; he's a turkey farmer in England. Farm-to-table is popular in the U.S. but it's not a concept that's taken hold yet in the UK. John raises free-range turkeys and he's trying to expand his business. Mostly he sells fresh turkeys before

Christmas but he's entrepreneurial and learned a lot from visiting us in Seattle and then Montana.

Now he's planning to source Brussels sprouts from the farm next door and offer a combination turkey box with vegetables—the whole farm fresh experience—to Michelin star restaurants.

You never know where you'll get promotional ideas. John came to visit us and to get in some skiing at Big Sky. He noticed what farmers are doing here and is taking the packaging and branding concepts back with him.

I'm sure he'll start a trend in England.

Being open to new ideas could be your "aha" moment.

Bragging versus promoting

When my business partner and I first used to interview candidates, we spent most of the time telling them how our company was so great. We'd talk about all the things we had to offer. Then we would ask the candidate why he or she wanted to work with us.

In this process, we were setting ourselves up for failure. We were so proud of what we built that we wanted to share it with everyone. In doing so, we did ourselves a disservice for it was just plain bragging.

We should have used that same amount of effort to learn more about the candidates and what they had to offer us, plus how their personalities would fit within our culture. We had it a bit backward.

The same was true when we pitched new customers. We quickly learned to focus on the customers and their needs instead of talking about ourselves. Being good listeners helped us land new business and diversify our client base.

Worth its weight

The best advertisement and marketing is from former customers. Nothing helps a business more than a happy customer telling another potential customer how good you are. My own business was built from referrals. Make sure to focus on keeping your customers happy, delivering what you say you will, and keeping your costs under control. Referrals will follow.

Have you ever been to a doctor's office, sitting there for a long time wondering when you are going to be seen? Doctors are notoriously late for appointments, but if you show up only 15 minutes late for your appointed time, the receptionist wants to reschedule you.

Imagine if movie theaters were run this way. After you arrive to see a movie, the theater staff shows up 15 minutes late, and then they take another 15 minutes to get the movie started. You would probably never go back.

The lesson here is that people have options and choices. They can pick another place to do business. It's vital that you treat your customers with respect. Without customers, you have a failing business no matter how skilled you are.

Projecting positive energy is vitally important. More often than not, image becomes reality.

CHAPTER 8:

Managing Growth

"Management is doing things right; leadership is doing the right things."
—Peter F. Drucker, author and management consultant

"Good management consists in showing average people how to do the work of superior people."—John D. (Davison) Rockefeller, Sr., oil industry magnate

"Management is, above all, a practice where art, science, and craft meet."
—Henry Mintzberg, academic and author

"It can wait until Monday"

It was a Friday and one of my employees was at his father-in-law's funeral. Someone in my office was worried about a project scheduled for that day; she was texting the employee questions and he was responding from the funeral. I quickly asked her to stop texting him—some things are just more important than work. I told her to let the client know we'd have the work done on Monday instead.

If you set expectations and have the confidence to say, "No," everything will almost always work out. You can't operate out of fear that the work might go to someone else.

The truth is that people are reasonable, but they do have a need to know. I believe it's a matter of integrity. If I say we're going to do something, I'll make sure we do it. But if we can't do something, I'll inform the client. It's all about communication.

And if the delay is due to the client, I don't blame them for anything; I just reset expectations.

Resetting expectations

Those who have remodeled a house know it's either painful or fun depending upon your viewpoint. I personally love the outcome and even the process, but I hate the things that can go wrong, including delays and other disappointments.

Recently my husband Rex and I purchased our dream home in the Florida Keys. Our intent was to remodel it bit by bit. For some reason the previous owners put carpet in the bedrooms. In the Keys you need either tile or stone due to the dampness and humidity, so our first planned project was to replace the flooring.

We hired a company and were ready to start. Then we heard Hurricane Irma was headed our way. The construction company packed up and said they'd be back once the storm passed. We moved the deck furniture inside and thought we were good to go. Then category 4 hurricane forces hit our house and the roof was ripped off.

I had to adjust my timeline on getting the floor done. After six months, I still didn't have walls and the house had to be gutted. The floors were the least of our worries. To most this would seem like a disaster. Looking at the upside, since we were already working with a construction company, they made us a priority client. They were able to install a new roof for us the first week after the roads opened back up.

There's a lesson in this for those running a business. Relationships with suppliers can be invaluable when disaster strikes. Make sure to treat everyone right and often those you've hired before, or others in the universe, will return the favor.

Leading from strength

I can't tell how many times I've paddled like crazy to keep afloat while looking calm on the surface to everyone else. In the process, I've learned not to back down in difficult situations and not to let others intimidate me. It's easy to get intimidated, but you have to fight it.

People say I'm a strong leader and I believe they are right, though on the inside I don't always feel strong. I just don't show any hesitancy, any doubt.

One of my techniques is to over prepare so I don't get caught out and look weak. Education is a great way to be strong. Knowing more than others in the room puts you in a position of strength. Read more than the person next to you. Talk to more people and learn as much as you can in advance. Preparation is vital to managing and taking the lead in most business circumstances.

Listening to get ahead

When I started out in business, I used to talk more than I listened. Like many of us, I liked the sound of my own voice. As a result, I was a terrible manager who lacked patience and listening skills. I was easily frustrated and wanted to take on everything myself since I felt I could do all of it faster and better.

Eventually I grew as a manager and found it did take longer to train people than to do a task myself. But once someone was trained, I could be hands off. With this realization, I learned the art of delegation—an essential element in any successful leader.

The art of listening, on the other hand, was harder for me to learn. It was easy for me to get bored listening to many other people.

I would tune them out and start thinking about what I wanted to say next. To stay actively engaged, I got better at keeping people on track and on point so I could understand what they need. Now I don't waste their time or mine.

My colleague Noland and I have worked together for almost 20 years and we share an office. People come into our office all day long to talk to me and Noland knows whether I am listening or not. Occasionally I will hear him say, "You might want to repeat that. Sharon is not listening to you." That always gets my attention. Noland's remark reaches me and I immediately disengage from multitasking, focusing instead on the person or persons in front of me.

Underdogs

Being the underdog has its advantages. When others expect you to fail, it is much easier to succeed and do so on your own terms. This may sound counterintuitive, but it is true.

I can't count the number of times I've failed at something, but each time it set me up for later success. I simply love the idea that if you're not failing, you're not out there trying and doing things. I know I would not have the determination to be successful if I had not failed over and over again.

As a result, I'm not afraid of failure for I expect that things will not work out initially. Then I expect I'll need to figure out an alternative plan. I also expect I'll have to work harder than most people, but I don't mind as long as I win in the end.

I recently read Malcolm Gladwell's book, *David and Goliath: Underdogs, Misfits, and the Art of Battling Giants*. I love the book for I relate to being the underdog. I struggled in school, struggled to earn my college degree, and struggled to get several advanced degrees.

Schoolwork came easily to many of my friends and yet they are not as successful as I am, for they did not develop the skills that are needed to cope when things go wrong. After all, they were used to things working out. For me, things almost never went my way and I learned to expect them to go wrong. When they did go wrong, I simply coped and kept going.

I always wondered why my friends gave up sooner than me, and I seemed more motivated. After reading *David and Goliath,* I understand that life taught me the skills to cope. I am prepared for failure, which ultimately means I won't let failure get in my way.

Failure is just one path to success.

Lesson learned

Never think the people who work for you are your friends.

My Dad was running a company in the UK. Every month he would have his senior staff and their spouses over for dinner. My mother loved to entertain and she would go all out making these great dinners. My parents pulled out all the stops serving great wine and food.

By all accounts, the dinner parties should have been a great success. Yet years later, a former employee told my Dad they hated the monthly dinners. His wife dreaded going—she never felt comfortable and they always argued beforehand. He felt they had to go as part of his job.

My Dad thought he was doing something good for his staff. My Mum went out of her way to impress everyone. They did not realize that no one wanted to give up family time to spend one night a month with the boss and his wife. My Dad is still upset no one appreciated what they did for them.

I have made similar mistakes with my own employees. In one instance, I hired a woman near my age and thought we'd become friends. However, I quickly discovered all she wanted to do was talk negatively about the rest of the staff. Things went south pretty fast as she became one of the most difficult employees I ever hired. She was inflexible, an unreasonable perfectionist, and continuously nasty about her co-workers.

Though she did her job well, no one wanted to work with her. Eventually even I made the list of people who did not measure up to her expectations. She was the opposite of a team player and was certainly a liability. Luckily she quit before I had to let her go.

Bigger is better, sometimes

Overextending and overtaxing your resources by taking on too much too soon can derail your business. Success is exciting and exhausting all at once, and learning to manage success takes practice. Sometimes you need to turn things down in order to move forward.

Sometimes the right approach is limiting your growth so it is manageable. Though it is true that fast-growth companies may be held together with duct tape, the chance of things going wrong is much greater than if they took it more slowly.

Focus on forming the right business alliances too. You can bid on projects with another company in order to augment your firm's skills. You can also look for business matchmaking opportunities.

Initially I lacked a sales team, so I hired an organization that focused purely on sales and networking. I gave them directives as to who I wanted to target and had them set up the meetings. There are many great companies that provide off-site sales services.

Here one minute, gone the next

I've missed opportunities by not being ready. It took me too long to respond, turn my head, or just see the opportunity.

What I learned is to always work on my business connections. If an opportunity comes along that I cannot handle by myself, I can bring in a team to help me. Plus, if I truly can't do the work, I can share the business with someone else. The other business owner may do the same for me at a later date, but I don't expect or count on it.

There are three types of people—takers, givers, and equalizers. We all recognize a taker—someone who takes advantage of every opportunity and leaves you feeling like you lost something. Givers can't stop giving their time and support but often grow resentful when no one helps them in return. And yet, givers keep volunteering for everything.

Equalizers value give and take. If you do something for them, they will do something for you. They don't want to owe anyone anything.

For years I tried to collaborate on projects with other companies, hoping we would become partners. We bid on a few joint opportunities, but we never quite landed any of the deals.

I always walked away feeling like I wished it had worked. Having two completely different perspectives would have been fantastic. I never let the loss of opportunity change my desire to keep trying.

Timing really is everything

I have been on the end of good timing and bad timing. My skills did not change, my offerings did not change, but the need for them did. If you keep yourself visible without being too pushy people will be reminded you do something they need and they will reach out to you.

However, if you get too pushy they are going to avoid you. It is a balancing act and you have no control over timing.

What you *can* do is be prepared to act. Whether it is being ready to make a change when the market changes, or seeing what people need and being available to them at the right time and place, preparation is done ahead of time. Taking action is what you do when the opportunity presents itself.

Focus, focus, focus

Entrepreneurs are already working on their next idea before you can finish reading this sentence. That is both a plus and a minus. There is no lack of opportunities, just a lack of time to realize them.

Staying focused on what you plan to do is really hard. Sometimes you need someone else to help you with this.

Get a mentor and use as many professional resources as you can. Most successful businesses have an advisory board or a board of directors to provide an outside perspective. Plus a board will keep you accountable.

An advisory board can also bring in skills that you are lacking. These can include specific talents and contacts.

A lot of people are hiring business coaches too. If you take this route, just make sure to get advice from the right type of coach who can actually help you achieve your goals. Remember the old saying, "You get what you pay for."

The all-important road map

Have a plan. It doesn't matter if your plan changes or gets updated. But it *is* important to know what you are trying to achieve. You don't need to know all the details in advance, but you should have an idea how to get from point A to point B so you can accomplish your goals.

There are some great tools for building business plans. Don't pay someone else to do this for you because you need to be the one to think through the process and understand the competition. You also need to know what you are trying to do and how you think you are going to get there. Your plan does not need to turn out to be right. It just needs to be there and then you can change it as events warrant.

If you don't formulate business goals, you can't take action on those goals every day. If you don't share those goals with anyone, no one else will be there to help achieve them. People always say to surround yourself with smart people. I say surround yourself with smart people with whom you can communicate and bring them to the table.

Hiring right matters

As you grow a company, you have to grow the management of the company. It is just the same as if you move up in an organization—you need to adapt your management style.

The biggest transition for me was learning to work *on* the business and not *in* the business. I was used to doing projects, meeting deliverables, and working within the team. However, my team members did not need me to roll up my sleeves. What they needed me to do was figure out what came next. The best thing I could do for everyone was to let go of what I knew how to do and manage from above.

What ultimately helped me grow the business was hiring the right team. Don't think for a minute that selecting the right employees isn't hard work, but know that it's well worth the effort.

Interviewing people effectively is an important skill. From past experience I know that the people I immediately like don't always turn out to be the best for the job. However they are the best at interviewing.

When hiring, it helps if you have good clear job descriptions. Knowing what any job entails, and what is needed to perform that job, is the key to hiring the right individual to fill that role. Also knowing how well the applicant will interact with clients and other team members can make a big difference on that hire's success.

Beyond first impressions

At one point we hired a new sales director—a difficult position to fill.

Salespeople are typically good at interviewing; after all, that is what they do—they convince you to buy something. In the interview process, they are convincing you to buy their services.

My partner and I interviewed four candidates after first screening the dozens of applications we received.

The fourth person who interviewed came into the office and for whatever reason, I decided within just ten minutes that he was not right for us. To my surprise, he proceeded to convince me he was just what we needed. I was ready to send him away but he skillfully got me to focus, pay attention, and look beyond my first impression.

I am turned off by people who are too friendly or overly familiar on the first meeting. But it turns out this sales director is a super friendly person—he just loves meeting and talking to everyone.

If I let my bias get in the way, we would not have hired him and we would have lost out, for he was great at generating sales.

Hire the best person for the job, not the best job seeker.

No matter how well you are prepared or how great your services, timing can't be controlled. Just be ready to catch onto the next opportunity.

CHAPTER 9:

Looking and Feeling the Part

"No one ever made a difference by being like everyone else."—P.T. Barnum, showman and founder of Barnum & Bailey Circus

No *Eat, Pray, Love*

Since you're reading this book, I'm going to guess you don't view *Eat, Pray, Love* as your new bible. It's a brilliant book and inspires many people to become more spiritual. However, I do not agree with its premise for I struggle with people who think they should only do things about which they are passionate.

As kids, lots of people want to be park rangers. After all, it's an often glamorized role requiring toughness and grit to survive outdoors and help others overcome difficult terrain, wild animals, and the elements. But the reality is that it's hard to support yourself, not to mention a family, on a park ranger's salary. That doesn't mean it can't be done or that you shouldn't do it. I still find it has a strong romantic appeal.

But reality means that sometimes we have to do jobs like accounting or manufacturing—jobs that don't excite us quite so much as working outdoors in the forest—in order to pay the bills and feed our families.

It's important to enjoy what you do, of course, but sometimes work is a means to an end—buying us the necessities as well as the leisure to enjoy our lives outside work. Work should not be everything and it should not necessarily be the most important thing. Family, friends, sports, interests—in other words, life—should take precedence and be what you love most.

I use my weekends and other times off to do the things I love. I don't have to spend eight hours a day at work doing something I love. I like what I do and I'm good at it, but I'm not entirely passionate about it all the time. I lose momentum. I gain momentum. I'm disconnected and reconnected. It is just *part* of life.

I know a wonderful woman who is driven to always do something spiritual that fulfills her. I believe she loves the book *Eat, Pray, Love* so that's why it came to mind. She can't imagine working at a job she's not passionate about so she doesn't always work. The irony is that she frequently asks for money to support her passions. She sees herself as a free spirit whereas when I look at her, I see someone who needs a full-time job. It's all about your perspective.

If you are like me, you need to be independent with a financial path that does not involve using other people's money.

My journey

Necessity is a strong motivator. When I started out, I got fired from numerous jobs before I found a career path that satisfied me and for which I am suited.

Prior to my becoming a business owner, I was a lifeguard, waitress, bartender, cleaner, rat runner (for a day in a research facility), and counselor.

Then I started working in more relevant occupations—statistician, adjunct professor, usability specialist, program manager, marketing manager, business consultant, speaker, vice president, and eventually business owner.

Instead of being in a position where I can possibly get fired, I now pay people to work for me, which is my best option. I am not unique in having found my entrepreneurial spirit after being fired from more than one job.

My being an entrepreneur also has a lot to do with lessons I learned at home from my parents.

Family is important

Risk-taking is part of my DNA—in my genes from both sides of my family.

Dad was from a coal miner's family in Derbyshire, England. He was one of seven children and he joined the British Royal Navy when he was 18.

He met my Mum, who was originally from Scotland. They met in Malta where she was living because my grandfather was in the Royal Air Force (RAF) and he was stationed there.

Mum was from a risk-taking family too and she was always looking to get ahead. She worked at many different jobs, including as a personal assistant for the British Embassy in Iran.

I was born in Fareham, a town on the southern coast of England. That's where my Dad was stationed with the British Royal Navy when I came along. A large fleet is based there.

As a child, I lived in many different countries, including Libya, Iran, Morocco, Scotland, England, Wales, and the United States.

Once Dad got out of the Navy, he took a job as a communications specialist in Libya and we went with him. That was at a time just before Gaddafi was in power. The Italians left and when the coup was imminent, we were evacuated as a family by the British government.

Our suitcases had already been packed for weeks. My Mum had packed all her cocktail dresses. I focused on toys and my brother made sure to take his model airplanes.

Soldiers were in the street and tanks were rolling down the road. As kids, we were not allowed to play outside and when bombing occurred, I remember going to the supermarket and finding a large hole in the floor where all the potato chips had fallen. I wondered why it couldn't have destroyed some other area of the store, not the precious chips!

My father was resourceful and he made sure we were all ready to go. He had also set up communication with other houses so that everyone in our community was informed and ready.

That was one of the numerous times we went back to Scotland to live. Scotland was home base where my maternal grandparents lived in a magical place (to me) called Dura Den outside the town of Cupar in the region of Fife. We stayed with our grandparents in their old stone mill house on the river.

Living in other countries and having these kinds of experiences, you grow up fast and develop independence and self-reliance. It's also valuable to learn to understand different cultures, a skill which I later parlayed into understanding diverse companies and personalities. To me, recognizing and adjusting to differences is just normal.

Growing up

My parents sent me to boarding school when I was 10 along with my brother who was 11. We thrived and learned how to adapt while spending weekends with our grandparents and aunts.

We even became expert at navigating travel around the world. For instance, we learned to wait until all the other passengers checked in at the airport. Then we would show up looking lost; 75 percent of the time this got us upgraded along with a trip to visit the cockpit.

We didn't have a lot of money as a family, which was okay because my Mum was frugal when she had to be and she made it work. As a kid, I remember standing in front of the butcher shop with my Dad. He wanted a leg of lamb for Sunday roast. Mum, on the other hand, wanted material so she could make bedroom curtains.

They could only afford one or the other—the lamb or the curtains. Mum was strong-willed and she won out.

My Mum was also one of the bravest people imaginable. She took her small children—my brother and me—with her into the war zones of Libya and later Tehran.

She was also incredibly brave when she was diagnosed with breast cancer at the age of 48 and again at 53 when she was given only two months to live. Five years earlier she was given the "all clear" but it came back in her whole body. She matter-of-factly made sure to see everybody and put things in order. She is my role model on how to be brave.

Dad encouraged Mum's strength, as he's also done with me throughout my entire life. Though he's from an era when women were less front and center in the workforce, my Dad has always liked strong women and he's totally supportive of my career and businesses.

I'm definitely a combination of both parents. From Dad I get motivation, ambition and stubbornness. He is always about trying different things and pushing to get things done. From Mum I get my strong-willed independence. My brother is obviously a product of them too. He's super smart and has his own way of doing things; he doesn't conform, instead finding and implementing creative solutions. His skills as a plastic surgeon are life-changing and amazing.

Be careful what you wish for

I always wished I was in charge. I wanted to be the one making decisions, taking the credit, running the show. What I did not count on was the toll it would take on my health.

I can't say I got fat as I was never in super shape to begin with. Let's just say I got fluffier. My blood pressure went up. My cholesterol went up. And my self-esteem went down. My pants got bigger out of necessity and I lost sleep. I even had a few moments when I had panic attacks and thought I could not breathe.

How is someone who can start, build and sell a company unable to stick to an exercise plan and diet? Well, that's me. I focus on doing things for others and have a hard time putting myself first.

In fact, I even signed up for one of those expensive weight loss programs where you get weighed in weekly and have to track your food. Though I continue to pay for the program, I never go to a meeting or a weigh-in. Who does that?

The funniest moment came when I hired my personal trainer as a project manager in my company and started him on a new career path. He loves the opportunity. Unfortunately, I am still fluffy.

So ladies and gents, make sure you stay or get healthy. I have to constantly remind myself the most important asset worth looking after is me, myself and I. You know the important directive, "Put your own oxygen mask on before helping others."

I'm still paying for the weight loss program on my credit card. It is way past time I just admit I'm never going—I must have signed up in the 1990s. I simply need to back away from the table, put on some good sneakers, and start walking in any direction.

Health and appearances matter

If I threw a stone into a room full of entrepreneurs, I would hit someone who is battling a health issue. It's obvious that forging any worthwhile path you are going to have some really big ups and downs—both in business and personally. You need to be prepared to take on these fluctuations of fortune.

I recently attended an event sponsored by the group Women in Technology. It was wonderful to see so many people excited about the future. On the way out from one of the talks I met a nice woman; she was wearing a flannel shirt and old jeans. We started talking in the elevator and eventually sat down for a chat.

I told her I love helping people who are starting out on a new course. She told me she was fed up with her job. She was planning to quit, take a break and take time off. I looked at her and said, "Are you nuts?"

Here are my reasons:

First, she was in her forties but she looked fifty plus—she had run out of energy. One look at her and I knew if she came to me for a job, I'd have a hard time hiring her and putting her in front of my clients.

Second, if she quit her job without lining up another one, she would probably be out of work for a while.

Third, from our brief talk, she did not appear up-to-speed on current technology.

Fourth, she did not have enthusiasm and that came through her posture, looks, and overall negative energy.

I recommended she work on polishing her skills and taking advantage of being employed by using her connections to look for another job.

If she had gotten her wish of taking time off, I think it would have ended up lasting a lot longer than the amount of time for which she was bargaining. I am making assumptions, but people judge you in less than a minute and I spent several minutes with her.

By the way, I saw her the next day and she was wearing a flannel shirt again and the same dirty jeans. I really wanted to recommend a makeover but felt that would be unkind.

All-important style

Everyone has heard the term, "dress for success," even me. Not that I paid much attention to it. That is, until I met an impressive personal stylist.

I was invited to attend a workshop arranged by one of my entrepreneur friends who has a clothing business. She had a personal stylist on hand to give us tips on how to dress. The man was 6' 4" and really well put together with a presence that was hard to ignore. He gave his presentation about dressing and clothes and I said to myself, "Yeah, yeah, yeah." In my mind I already had style and looked good.

The stylist gave each person at the event a free five-minute evaluation. I used my time to pitch him on how I could fix his brand and make his marketing materials match his look. I said, "Your presentation material is terrible and you are not showing your true skills."

He was just starting out so I said I would work a trade with him. I would fix his brand and he would do an image consultation with me. This consultation involved going through my closet, getting rid of everything that looked bad, making me a list of basics, and taking me shopping for new clothes. I was certain his time would be wasted and on this basis I agreed.

The stylist arrived at my house with two personal assistants. Of course, I had already been through my closet and hidden all the clothes I thought he would throw out. Part of the rules he set included his leaving with all the things that did not work on me if they were not a good fit, needed repair, or were just plain wrong.

Well, four hours later he left with seven trash bags full of clothes. Plus he told me my hair was too out of control; I needed to look more polished. I love my hair. It *is* wild and crazy. I fumed for days.

The experience was humbling and really made me look at myself the way others see me. And I learned a lot about myself. I was used to hiding my body behind baggy clothes, never trying anything on in a store and just purchasing everything on the assumption it would fit.

Upon self-reflection, this taught me I was afraid to feel bad if things did not fit. I now know that all my clothes were two sizes too big and I was shopping at the wrong stores. The stylist took me to a few stores and introduced me to brands I could wear off the rack. Next he taught me that nothing is right just off the rack—everything worth buying needs to be fitted. I hired someone to start taking in all my clothes.

I learned to appreciate my best features and got my hair done with a keratin treatment that tames my curls and gives me a polished look. I even had facial rejuvenation work done that makes me look ten years younger.

We made a fabulous website and logo for the stylist, and did all his branding. His business is thriving and I still think about the impact he had on me. Though I was reluctant at first, I certainly became a convert.

It's important to put your best look forward and not neglect how you look for it makes quite a difference in how you are perceived. As an added bonus, you might actually be like me and feel better for it.

Always make sure to look the part.

Red jacket strategy

My Mum always told me to buy the best I can when it comes to shoes and purses, that a good presentation is improved with accessories.

I've also learned I have the ability to do a fabulous job so I don't have to conform. That's why I always wear red. In this way I really stand out. After all, I'm the person in the red jacket.

Red is bold and colorful. If it's not a red jacket, I'll wear a white dress with big red flowers all over it. I just make sure I'm the brightest one in the room.

Former U.S. Secretary of State Madeleine Albright used to always wear a statement pin. She was known for this and it was a way to start a conversation. Many commentators would wonder which pin she was going to wear for a particular occasion.

Don't be afraid to stand out and don't try to blend in. If you carry yourself like you're sure of yourself, people will be impressed. Wearing a bold color—whether red or yellow or bright green—will ensure your presence is noticed.

This matters for men too. In place of shoes and purses, there are watches, colorful ties and of course, well-made and well-shined shoes.

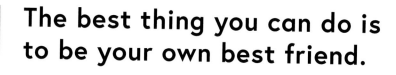

The best thing you can do is to be your own best friend.

CHAPTER 10:

Flexibility is Key

"What I wanted was to be allowed to do the thing in the world that I did best—which I believed then and believe now is the greatest privilege there is. When I did that, success found me."—Debbi Fields, of Mrs. Fields cookie fame

Inflexibility is a deal breaker

Everyone talks about the "gray ceiling"–when you get older it is hard to get a job or land a project. The preference often goes to those younger, less costly, and in their prime. Older applicants are seen as past their prime.

Much of this is no doubt true, but equally true is that many people become more and more inflexible as they get older and less willing to take risks; they tend not to do things outside their comfort level. It can even become a battle to get him or her to turn their head.

Don't let this happen to you.

Stay flexible no matter what.

Did you really want this job?

I had one employee who came back to work after taking several years off to raise her children. Her kids were now older and in school, so she wanted to return to the workforce. She should have been a great fit. After all, she knew my company well and had been good at her work in the past. She was likable too.

However, she informed me that in order to take a job with me, I had to accommodate *her* schedule and work around *her* needs. I had a business to run and that just did not work. It's one thing to be reasonable and understanding of an employee; it's another to have them make unrealistic demands. She even wanted to work from home just to avoid paying a toll to go over a bridge on the way to the office.

Working from home is feasible when you are established and have a clear set of goals or deliverables. But when you are jumping back into the workforce, you have catching up to do and will benefit from being around other team members. Eventually it might have made sense and she could certainly have expressed a desire to work toward that goal. However, demanding it happen right away and making it a deal breaker when she supposedly wanted a job, just didn't make sense.

Needless to say, I didn't re-hire her. Last I heard she is still unemployed. She gave up a good job with me over a $4 toll. She gets to stay home but her inflexibility killed a perfect opportunity for her to go back to work. I don't even think she knows she was inflexible. She just wanted things a certain way—her way. That's fine sometimes. It wasn't in this case.

Personal relationships

I apologize to my single friends for what I am about to say. But inflexibility is one of the reasons you are still single. It's not because all the good people are taken. Lots of good people find themselves back in the dating market for a number of reasons.

Flexible people willing to step outside their comfort zones tend to meet more people. And dating, like many other activities, is a numbers game. The more people you meet, the more likely you are to find a connection.

Be brave

I met my husband on a sailboat race in Canada. I took up sailboat racing because it scared the hell out of me and I found it took every ounce of concentration to do even a tiny little job onboard. I was not used to that kind of fear and I was determined to conquer it. I volunteered on a crew and just showed up every week. I soon learned I had to go with the flow and break out of my comfort zone to succeed.

People shouted at me when I was clueless. One captain wanted me to release the mainsheet since the boat was tipping quite far over. I was thinking, 'What the hell is the mainsheet?' He just kept shouting over and over again and louder and louder.

I finally told Captain Bligh that no matter how loudly he shouted I did not know what he wanted. He then said, "Could you let out that line to the left of you a bit?" I did and the line partially loosened the mainsail, stopping the boat from tipping over and everyone was happy.

My husband was on that crew. He thinks I am the bravest scaredycat he has ever met.

Trying something different

The biggest lesson I learned in business is that if you don't try something different, you are just going to be like everyone else. And if whatever you try doesn't work, you should just try something else.

Whether you run a business or work in a corporate environment, embracing flexibility is going to matter. Whether you are changing your business model, adding new solutions, updating your pricing, or just being innovative—the importance of flexibility cannot be overvalued.

Big clients gladly hire smaller firms to help with non-critical business components. They know smaller firms are nimble and better able to do things quickly.

If you run a small firm, you just have to make sure to deliver the best quality product or solution around. It's important to have the capability to mold and change your offerings so you can deliver the results your customers need. Couple this flexibility with high quality and you can earn market share even in the most saturated niches. Providing something no one else offers will solidify your offerings even more, earning you a much bigger piece of the market.

Microsoft who?

While I was working on my Ph.D. dissertation, Microsoft recruited me to apply my knowledge about software design and usability to their products. This was during a time when User Experience Design was new and fresh; and it was also the start of my professional path.

In the 1990s, I had never heard of Microsoft, so it ended up a nice surprise when it turned out to be an excellent company. Working for Microsoft was a great ride filled with lots of highs and I got the opportunity to work on some awesome products.

After Microsoft, I joined first one start-up and then another. The first one sold cell phones online and turned out to be a total flop. The second one grew into one of the biggest travel sites in the world.

One out of two is a great track record in the world of tech start-ups and I'm proud of my part in advancing the travel site.

Assessing strengths and weaknesses

After the start-ups, I worked at two consulting firms. This experience made a significant impact on my ability to open and run my own business. Though consulting and running a business are different skills, there is definitely crossover.

Let me explain what I mean. As a consultant, you advise clients in your area of expertise. You are generally paid by the hour and you are an outsider with a strong motivation to ensure your client's success. Lots of times you are hired to fix a problem or series of problems.

Sometimes you are hired to improve a product or service, or to give guidance on scaling the business. Scaling is when a company decides to take the next step into substantially enlarging the operation.

Running a business is obviously different than being an independent consultant. As a business owner or manager, you need to pay rent, hire employees, file taxes, handle human resources (HR), find customers, provide customer service, create or sell products and services, and much, much more.

Getting back to my personal experience, the first consulting firm where I worked was Paperless Business Systems at their subsidiary Elephants and Ants. Working at Paperless I learned the importance of the bottom line. The owner was great at keeping control over the financial aspects of the company. From him, I learned some valuable lessons.

The other consulting firm where I worked was Inviso where I learned about strategy and techniques for building out new lines of business. The owners were fabulous and I only left because I wanted to become a business owner myself. I still follow their success and I'm pleased to have helped them at their start. We have since become competitors for some projects and I am proud to be playing on the same field as Inviso.

Rabbit holes

Whether it's fear of failure, fear of success, fear of the unknown, or fear of leaving a paycheck—we all have it.

Yet despite this, I sold my stable business and started on a new path right when things were particularly challenging. I was in the middle of remodeling my home from extensive hurricane damage. I was also updating a rental property. Money was tight to say the least. As a consultant, I only had one new client along with lots of fear that I had made the wrong choice by selling my company.

I did all this to try something new and challenge myself again. Thankfully there was no turning back, for it all worked out. But I was scared.

Always keep in mind that doubts are normal. Getting stuck in your head or going down a rabbit hole in your thinking is what stops you from moving forward.

I was talking to a successful business owner the other day as she created all sorts of scenarios why something she is doing in her business will fail. She focused on all the worst-case scenarios until I reminded her that none of them might happen.

Building a business or taking on a new role is exciting and scary all at once. So don't be like Alice in Wonderland falling into a rabbit hole.

You've probably come across business owners who do just what it takes to succeed. They believe in their ideas and businesses. They make mistakes, but they don't stop when they run into issues. You just need determination.

Someone very dear to me quits every time something gets hard—throws in the towel and walks away whether it's merely a broken-down car or a job where someone challenges him. When I look at his family dynamics, I find he comes by this behavior honestly. It's how his entire family reacts so he learned firsthand how to quit. Keep in mind that how you behave will influence your daughters and sons too.

On the other hand, I was lucky for I learned from my parents and grandparents to never to give up on things that are important. Instead just find a different way to succeed.

I've heard others say about me, "Oh she had it easy." But nothing could be further from the truth. I've had to try, fail, and then try again. The truth is when you are successful no one knows what it took to get there. The more difficult lesson for me is learning when to recognize success myself. Like many, I continue to compare myself to people who are out of my league.

It's important to remember there will always be someone out there who is richer, thinner, or more famous than you. Knowing you are successful and feeling it does not mean comparing yourself to everyone else in the universe, especially to rock stars and billionaires.

You're the only one who should gauge your success. If you're getting ahead, meeting and surpassing goals, and progressing in a way that makes you happy, you're doing well. Better than well—you're doing great.

Encouraging others to take initiative

As women, we really need to encourage other women to succeed. There are misperceptions that women who want to get ahead are selfish and being ambitious is seen as negative. Men don't seem to have this problem.

For all of us, being powerful, ambitious, and financially secure are fantastic goals. We should encourage others to get ahead too. We can use our connections to help the women (and men) we know reach their vision even as we're striving to reach our own.

One of my favorite successful women is Suze Orman. One Saturday morning I found myself watching an infomercial on her secrets to wealth. She told the story of how she got started and it's a great story. She failed her first time around when she let someone invest $50,000 for her and they lost it all. That experience started her on the path to money management. She did a better job herself and after that, she soared.

Now she spends her time educating and helping others take the initiative. She does not have to do this, but she is driven to help people stop feeling powerless. Suze is one of my heroes.

Skills different from your own

When most people set up their businesses, they don't engage professional services. Companies exist so you can now go online, fill in legal forms easily, and start a business. It is actually a great resource. People try to handle their own accounting and taxes too. Then they decide to add marketing and creativity to the list of things they do.

All these things you do yourself without engaging experts will cost you more in the long run. It is much harder to fix something than it is to do it right from the start.

Even when you do things properly, stuff happens. A woman I know is going through a horrendous legal battle due to the name of her company. She received a cease and desist letter from a large company saying she is producing products under a name too similar to theirs. Though the woman has a legal trademark, the company is going after her anyway.

This is a case of the bottom line ultimately mattering. The woman I know has to liquidate her company as it's too expensive to fight the large corporation.

Though she has a legitimate trademark, hiring the right defense team for a protracted fight would cost more than her company is worth. She has to be flexible, look at the long run, and walk away from the business. No doubt she'll start another one, for she inherently knows how to roll with the punches.

 # Trees that bend in the wind rarely break.

CHAPTER 11:

Creativity and Positive Thinking

"They will always tell you that you can't do what you want to do, but you can do what you want to do. You just have to believe in yourself. The system is to bring you down, but you can rise up."—Bob Marley, singer-songwriter

Strength in self-actualization

People can spend a whole lifetime trying to figure out their self-worth. Unless you are lucky enough to be surrounded by supportive people who make you believe you can do anything, it is up to you to do that for yourself.

Of course, it is never too late to find people who will encourage you. And it's a good idea to learn what motivation works best for you. Is it someone telling you can't achieve something? Is it proving something to your partner, co-workers or former boss?

It doesn't matter what motivates you, just so you develop the habit of believing in yourself.

If you don't believe in yourself, how can your boss, direct reports, co-workers, clients or employees believe in you?

Confidence you'll persevere

As an entrepreneur, you are going to experience a loss or setback at some point. If this has not happened yet, rest assured it will.

Being ready to fail at times is what prepares us for success. It's important to regularly count your wins, reminding yourself you are ready to deal with whatever stresses are inherent to failure. And it's good to know you'll find a way to overcome whatever difficulties occur.

When you are confident, you get satisfaction from what you do rather than relying on what others think of your accomplishments. And when you have confidence, you listen more than you speak. As a result, you learn a lot about a situation or task.

When you are confident you seek out new opportunities instead of fearing them.

Have you noticed that confident leaders are masters of attention diffusion? When someone gives them a compliment, these self-assured leaders move the focus to other people who helped make it happen. These leaders don't crave approval or praise; instead they draw their self-worth from within.

You can learn to be a confident person. The power of positive belief is amazing.

Ambition

Since you can nurture ambition in children, it's logical you should be able to do the same in adults. After all, nurturing fosters creativity, imagination, and emotional growth.

Entrepreneurs are creative by nature for they are always forming something new that has value. Creative play as a child develops creative thinking and it does for adults as well. Thus it's smart to engage in activities that cause you to think, whatever your age. You never know when or where your next new idea will occur.

I got to a point in my life where I felt stuck. I lost a job I liked along with the social connections that came with it. I felt ashamed I was being forced out of the position, so I quit to try and keep some of my dignity. I was no longer valued for my skills when the goals of my team changed.

The funny thing is that I was too creative for the team. Suddenly they valued different skills than mine and in the process, I felt like a failure. It took me years to be okay with what happened, but it resulted in leading me to greater things and it fueled my ambition to get ahead on my own.

At the time I had no hobbies or distractions to make me happy. My world revolved around my job.

New interests and destiny

I needed a distraction so I learned to sail, which took me out of my comfort zone and demanded every bit of my concentration. It did not leave me time to feel sorry for myself because I was so out of my depth.

I fell into sailing by accident when a friend asked me if I crewed. I thought he meant crewing on a rowboat, which I had done and liked. I showed up at the specified location and noticed that the boats kept getting bigger and bigger as I walked along the dock. I kept thinking the rowboats must be at the end of the dock. Well, I got to the slip number and there was a sailboat. It turns out, I'd volunteered to crew on a race boat.

I took one giant step aboard while making a mental note to sign up for sailing lessons. Just the act of learning something totally new changed my perspective. I developed additional friends and expanded my relationships. In the process, I got my confidence back and started to value small wins instead of focusing on what I perceived as large losses.

I was terrible at sailing when I started out, but I did not let that stop me. I just showed up every week for practice and found that was more than most people did. Most people are resistant to learning and trying new things, but knowledge is at the core of success.

Successful people want to learn everything and never stop improving themselves. Successful people create and innovate. They can change the world.

What makes success special is that it is hard to achieve. A lot of successful people work their way up from the bottom. Timing may play a part in their success, but they had to be present to take advantage of the timing.

Ambition plays a role too. You can depend on skills, but ambition is going to dictate whether or not you get where you're trying to go. If you are willing to sacrifice everything to get to the position you want, you'll probably achieve it.

The bottom line is you have to be prepared to work hard.

I have met some truly ambitious and successful people. Not all of them are nice; not all of them give back or share. When you achieve success and even when you're on the way up, don't lose sight of how you can make things better for others. The reward of helping others is special in its own right.

Psychology of risky actions

We all know someone who is an adrenaline junkie. That is the person who spends the weekend speeding around a racetrack or kiteboarding in a storm—a person who simply loves the feel of an adrenaline rush. But just because you don't engage in these types of risky activities does not mean you are not a risk-taker. You may get your rush from other, less obvious, but still risky behaviors.

You might also think that if you worry excessively you are not a risk-taker. Some research actually shows that people who score high on a neuroticism scale with a combination of anxiety, moodiness and worry are more likely to be risk-takers rather than less likely. This is not conclusive data, but it certainly makes one think. And yet other research shows the opposite, with risk-takers scoring lower on measures of neuroticism than the general population.

In either case, your personality is going to affect your risk-taking ability. Someone who smokes might be afraid of scuba diving with sharks but is willing to ignore the known health risks of smoking. Culture and peer pressure play a large part in risk-taking too. You're much more likely to take risks in a group setting than when you're alone.

The consequences of some risky behaviors are definitely not worth the dangers. But in small doses, risk-taking is good for mental health. Trying something new can reinvigorate you or revive a relationship.

And if you are an entrepreneur, risk-taking is necessary. After all, the excitement that derives from not knowing what is going to happen produces a natural high. As a result, risk-taking creates positive moods, which help lead to success. When you feel good about your business acumen, you tend to make wiser decisions.

Brainstorming

When I hear the word "brainstorming," I cringe.

I've been trapped in rooms where we have all been told to brainstorm and all I can think about is, "What am I having for lunch?" Brainstorming on demand just doesn't always work for me. At the right times, however, it's extremely useful.

Who you brainstorm with is just as important as the art of brainstorming. And there are lots of techniques for brainstorming that help you become more creative. Use whatever you need. Just start learning how to engage with others and how to accept feedback.

If you can't share your ideas and accept criticism from others, you are probably not going to be as successful as you could be.

"Gold! Gold! Gold! Gold!"

A Seattle newspaper ran this headline on July 17, 1897, heralding the thousands passing through the city on their passage to Alaska in search of striking it rich.

The Klondike Gold Rush was a boon for Seattle businesses and workers. It created a huge opportunity for new businesses to grow and outfit would-be miners, as well as handling the transportation for those miners to and from Alaska.

The Seattle businesses did nothing innovative, but they were the first to support what was needed during the gold rush. Few people struck it rich but businesses in the supply chain thrived.

To succeed, remember to sell the highest quality shovel or one for the lowest possible price—whatever your spin, just make sure to be good at it.

Deliver quality if you want to reap great rewards.

Study versus action

Women have a tendency to spend more time researching and reading about something before they try it, whereas men will often say, "Who needs a manual?"

As women, we want to follow directions, whereas a large percentage of men have enough confidence to assume they will be able to figure things out. Women should take a page from the men's playbook. Sometimes we just need a spot of courage. After all, we have the skills.

It's a fact that girls consistently outperform boys in the classroom and even at the university level. There is ample data to demonstrate the differences.

However, studies also show that ten years after college graduation, the gender gap in pay is around 23 percent less for women than men. Research shows the discrepancy may stem from women who undervalue themselves. Women are notoriously terrible at asking for raises and don't apply for new jobs unless they believe they are completely qualified. That doesn't usually stop a man.

I saw a cartoon recently with the caption something like, "Don't let my qualifications get in the way of your overconfidence." The illustration showed a woman sitting at a table with a man. He was dominating the conversation though she was the one with the skills.

I recently had something like this happen to me. I was presenting to a potential client. When he asked me a question, a team member in the meeting jumped in with an answer even though he had no clue what he was talking about.

I was the one with the expertise—not this person who made up a response just to sound clever. I had to say I disagreed, followed up by the actual answer.

It's not always easy to disagree but it's important to take a stand.

Don't let other people trample on your toes.

Anticipating the future

I tend to mentally play out what will likely go wrong before I take risks.

Right now I am working with clients on how to grow their businesses, helping to set them up for the next stage in their growth. It is easy to look at someone else's world and see the flaws. Though people don't want to hear about the negative aspects of things, I know it is good to plan for things that might go badly. I always try to present this information with a soft touch.

My husband would drive without wearing a seatbelt if not for the annoying noise pinging in the background. On the other hand, I am all about safety first so I buckle up right away. I suppose opposites really do attract.

It's wise to have a business partner who is the yin to your yang—someone with whom you can bounce ideas. If my husband Rex thinks something is risky, then it will pretty much land you in jail.

I surround myself with people who complement my skills and help me tackle my blind spots. If Rex was about to jump off a cliff, I'd make sure he had a working parachute on first. We really do complement each other.

Drive

Growing up, I got to watch my older brother, Steven, strive for his goals. He became a successful doctor and he's a hard act to follow.

I once had the pleasure of taking a client to my brother's office to spend the day shadowing him. We had to be there at 7 a.m. and I made sure we were earlier than that. I texted Steven and said we were in the lobby. He had already stopped at the hospital to see a patient on the way into the office.

Steven works incredibly hard. However, what sets him apart is his incredible drive and ambition. He is a perfectionist but that is an ideal trait in his profession. Whether in the operating room or in his hobbies, if Steven is going to do something, he jumps in with both feet.

When you are passionate about something, you have more drive. What is hard is having that same drive to do things that need to get done, but about which you are not so thrilled. Try tackling these things first and save the good stuff for later in the day when motivation is not at its highest.

There are many hard-working people out there. My brother has figured out how to maximize his time. The first thing he asked the physician who was shadowing him was, "How is your office set up?" He figured out what tasks she should hand off to other people and made those suggestions.

We all have the same number of hours in a day. How we use our time is important.

> **Not all risks are equal or worth taking. Make sure to consider those paths that have the greatest upside.**

CHAPTER 12:

Going Above and Beyond

"The difference between ordinary and extraordinary is that little extra."
—Jimmy Johnson, sports broadcaster and former football coach

"Perfection is not attainable, but if we chase perfection we can catch excellence."—Vince Lombardi, former football player and head coach of Green Bay Packers

"I'll bring the coffee"

In the service business, you don't need to be top dog; you don't need to take the credit. You just have to make sure the client is happy and gets what he or she needs.

If my hourly rate is $300 an hour and a client wants me to bring him a cup of coffee, I'll gladly stand in line at Starbucks to get him a latte at my hourly rate. It doesn't matter. I have a Ph.D. but I'll do it and I won't complain; it's not that important to me. Perhaps the client knows that with my education I'll get his order right.

Not everyone can do this and that's okay if it's not for you. But it's important that you develop a level of confidence in your abilities so the little things don't bother you.

As an entrepreneur, I can't expect my employees to do anything that I won't do. When my employees see me doing things, they jump up and say, "I'll do it," or "I'll help."

Be confident in your abilities and bring the coffee.

New ideas

It's hard to have a brand new idea or a more effective solution or process.

I have only been truly innovative a few times in my life, but I'm proud of those instances. While working as a usability expert at Microsoft in the late 1990s, my team was tasked with figuring out how to build a booking engine that could be used by people other than travel agents to book flights with a dial-up modem.

I was part of the design group that created the booking engine used by Expedia. My role was to develop a better method and process when things did not work. This was true innovation for the concept did not exist before we designed it.

Though dial-up modems are antiquated today, our booking engine model was copied by all the online booking travel sites and is still in use. The model has not changed. It was innovative when we created it, had utility, and is highly usable. It's exciting and rare when something you develop stands the test of time like this did.

Innovation can also grow from a desire to do something better or differently. After all, a spark often comes from the need to solve a problem. In the UK for example, it's common to have a roast with all the trimmings on Sundays. This is similar to Thanksgiving dinner here in the States only it occurs every Sunday in the UK.

One of my friends used to cut the ends off the roast before putting it in the oven. I watched her and wondered why she did this all the time. When I asked, she said her mother did it and her grandmother before her. With a bit more inquiry, we learned the family initially didn't have a roasting pan big enough for the meat. That is the exact opposite of innovation—at some point, they could have just purchased a bigger roasting pan!

But no one questioned their behavior or took the initiative to find a different solution. Just because something is done a certain way doesn't make it right. Innovation often grows out of a need to do things differently.

Learning to envision a better solution to an everyday problem can sometimes be your golden ticket in business. In one of my IT businesses, we built a tool to help us track financial data for one of our clients. We needed a better way to track projects other than a shared spreadsheet so we designed an innovative solution. We ended up rebranding the tool and selling it to many other clients for it served a widespread need.

Adding value

I hope my clients involve me in their projects because I add value, but that is not always true. Sometimes they ask me to do things they just don't want to do themselves. Either way, I am adding value.

One of the reasons I have been successful is that I don't mind how I add value. I just do it, even if I'm the one who is getting the coffee. If that's what it takes to keep everyone motivated and on task, then it's definitely worth it.

Many people have a need to get credit for a project's success. Though these individuals may not be the ones adding value, they definitely like to take the wins. You have to learn how to navigate around those people.

I don't have a big ego and as long as I know I've done the work, I don't need to be recognized. That is, unless money goes with the recognition—that's a different scenario. I wouldn't be a good businesswoman if I didn't insist on being properly compensated.

Becoming irreplaceable

Being essential is how you keep work and relationships going, but being vital to an operation is a double-edged sword. If you become irreplaceable, people love you as the glue that keeps a project together and they become reluctant to let you move on. When you're the top dog, you need others to let you go so you can delegate much of the work while you run the company.

As a business owner, on the other hand, it is bad when employees become irreplaceable for they may want to hold you hostage on the assumption that without them you won't have the account or the work. I had to learn the hard way that no one on my staff is irreplaceable. I now work hard to make sure no one holds a key to which I don't have a copy.

I had one employee who was starting on a great path to success. She was motivated, ambitious, outgoing and great with clients. In fact, she was getting a little too close to my clients. It's always best if clients belong to the business and not to an individual for an individual may leave. It's up to the business owner to make sure to have a connection too.

This employee called me one day and told me there was an opportunity to win another project with a particular customer. She said she was working on a bid to land the new work. It was all very exciting. Then she asked what I would pay her if she landed the extra business. I said we could discuss a raise but she wanted to know immediately and I said I'd have to think about it.

A few days later I asked how the bid went and the employee said we'd lost it. It turns out she had taken the contract to our competitor and put in a slightly lower bid for them to secure winning the business. In the process, she negotiated a new job at a higher salary for herself with the competitor.

I called the CEO of the competing firm and told him she violated her non-compete clause with us. He was appalled and thanked me for letting him know. She lost the new job and was still unemployed months later. My competitor and I agreed to check with each other going forward if anyone brings one of us a contract belonging to the other company's client, so I got a good business contact out of it.

Caring for employees

If you own or run a small business, it will be hard to compete for talent with the big dogs. You'll need to have something that appeals to job seekers.

In my company, this appeal was our work environment. It was a relaxed atmosphere and our employees really liked working for us. Most of the people we lost over time only left when we did not have a project for them or a career path that would take them to the next level.

When I sold the business, we held a party and invited all the former employees we could reach. They showed up *en masse* to tell me how great it had been working with us. Many gave me cards expressing gratitude for jumpstarting their careers. Others told me they missed the office and the great environment we created, making it one of their favorite places to work. Their sentiment was a compliment and reaffirmation that we had a great business.

It's smart to find out what motivates your team members. Each person may have a different motivation. I try and learn what each person needs and reward him or her with what they value most. For some it is having flexibility in their schedules. For others, they just want to make as much money as they can. Some individuals love working on a particular project or with a particular client.

Each is different but they all have one thing in common. They each want to be treated with respect, dignity, and to know they are valued. This seems simple but people let power trips get in the way and sometimes lose sight of these core values.

The extra mile

When you're running a marathon or even a sprint, it's the last bit of road or track that's often the hardest to finish.

Business is not that different. After spending months on a project, it's often the little extra you do at the end that will endear you to a client. Make sure you don't skimp at the last minute. You will be rewarded for tenacity with appreciation and future business.

People, product and process

According to the show *The Profit,* featuring Marcus Lemonis, these three pillars of your business all need to be strong:

The people on your team need to be stellar. The processes you have in place need to work like a charm. And the product (or service) needs to excel far above that of your competition.

This is how you succeed beyond your wildest imagination. This is how you take a start-up and turn it into a profitable, ongoing enterprise.

Faster, better and cheaper

One way to ensure success, or at least give yourself the clearest shot possible, is to stand out in your field. This entails getting and keeping a competitive advantage.

If speed is your firm's distinguishing characteristic, you'll likely get a lot of rush projects. Someone's got to work nights and weekends, and often a newly created firm takes on jobs established companies are willing to do but at prohibitive cost.

If you're better at something than the next guy or gal, customers will often spend more or wait longer for your skill. Talent and skill are excellent distinguishing characteristics.

Then there's price. Everyone cares about cost, right? Not really. If you can do the job faster and/or better, price is not always a factor. Then again, a majority of customers are cost conscious. However, if you provide a luxury product or service, high cost may be a badge of ego gratification for the customer.

Naturally, if you can handle a project faster, better, *and* cheaper, you'll likely get many contracts. That is, unless the decisive parameters include other variables such as previous experience, diversity or other certifications, the percentage of your firm's income represented by the contract, and other contingencies.

When bidding on a project, ask about the factors being used to award the contract. The more you know, the better your chances. Knowledge truly is power.

> **There's always more you can do. Calculate advantages and disadvantages, and then make your decisions.**

CHAPTER 13:

Implementing an Exit Plan

"Quit while you're ahead. All the best gamblers do."—Baltasar Gracian, philosopher

Planning ahead

Plan your exit from day one. This is the smart way to start, build and sell a business. You'll end up walking away while you still love it and you'll maximize your profits.

After all, there are many ways to exit your business and it's a sure thing that you'll do so eventually–one way or the other. The options are always there–quitting, dying, failing, going bankrupt, going public, or selling. There are variants and combinations of these options too.

The trick is to go out on your own terms–choosing your timing and methodology–the when and the how.

Things always occur that are outside your control. The world keeps moving, technology increases to an exponential extreme, nature has her revenge, political shifts take place, and legislation is passed and repealed.

You likely started or want to start a business so you can control your own destiny. To do so in the best way possible, you need to plan ahead, anticipating contingences, and flexibly reacting to those things outside your control.

Planning an exit strategy *is* within your control. Remember that!

Advice from a role model

I was invited to a friend's wedding in La Jolla, an affluent section of San Diego. The wedding ceremony was on a yacht and the after party was at this amazing home overlooking the Pacific Ocean. The compound had a couple of guest houses as well as the main house with a gorgeous bedroom for the owner.

When I had a chance, I asked the owner, "What did you do to become so successful? How did you get all this?" Luckily for me he shared his perspective.

He told me he started out as a barback running drinks and cleaning up for bartenders. He moved his way up the chain and bought his first nightclub at an early age.

"I figured out that people love restaurants and nightclubs that are new," he explained. "The secret to my success is that I look for a buyer and sell when a restaurant or club is going great. I sell the club for top dollar then open the next one, starting the hype all over again.

"In my business, the newest best thing is always hot. Once it's stagnant, it's too late. You need to sell when you're making the most money.

"Other people will say, 'But you're successful now. Why would you sell?' The answer is that you sell when everyone wants it.

"The public is fickle. If you stay too long, you need to start over. If I can't sell a restaurant, I'll totally change the design and menu, rebrand it and give it a new name. By gutting it and putting up a sign that reads, *Under New Management*, I can make it the next newest best thing."

That's how he had a $10 million property overlooking the beach and the Pacific. He knew when he loved his business the most, other people would want a piece of it—they would want to be part of his success.

Unfortunately, I listened but I didn't heed his lesson.

When my business was doing the best, I was too enthusiastic and just couldn't imagine selling at that point. It's definitely a catch-22 loving something so much and letting it go. I did sell and make money later, but I could have made much more.

Next time around, I'm going to plan on selling from day one.

For I know if I want the best result possible—to make the most money when selling a company—I'll plan to sell the first day I start it. By setting out to sell, I'll have an incredible incentive to get revenues up and keep costs down or at least keep them reasonable.

Upside of selling

There were many upsides to selling my business.

One, it gave me a tremendous sense of accomplishment. I started, built and now sold the business. That makes me feel like a success. No one else in my family has done all three. I truly feel like a winner, which is a wonderful way to feel. Plus, it gives me something new and exciting to talk about.

Two, it turns out that selling the business was arduous and in the process, I learned a great deal. I am glad to have that experience under my belt. It gives me a sense of power. I own this and I'm proud of it.

Three, the upside of selling is that it leaves my future unwritten. I was on one path for so long it became a part of me. Suddenly reaching the end of the path is quite exciting. I've never taken more than two weeks off between jobs or projects and suddenly I wasn't sure what I was going to do. That was exciting and scary all at once.

(Of course, I was already planning my next business. But the future was still undetermined.)

Four, it left a future for my treasured employees who were there for me when it counted and who I could not abandon. Instead of closing the business or staying and losing steam, I left only after I created a career path for them within the new company.

Given the nature of our business and their strong qualifications, if they don't like the new direction of the company, they have options elsewhere and I will still be around to help.

Looking out for employees

In some industries like IT marketing, employees generally stay at one firm for just a few years before moving on. So when I sold my business, I wasn't particularly worried about my employees since my company was an IT marketing and communications firm. All the people working for me are always on alert for their next opportunity anyway, so I knew they would be fine.

Still, I let them know I would do whatever I could to help them if they chose to leave under the new management.

In other businesses, longevity is much more prevalent. In these instances, it *is* necessary for the business owner to consider the fate of the company's employees as part of the equation when selling the business. This is not an absolute of course, for the owner doesn't have to do this.

However, it's good karma and ultimately good business. In a sense, it's equivalent to an employee making sure not to burn bridges with previous employers. An employer, especially a serial entrepreneur who will likely start her next business pretty quickly, may want the goodwill and services of former employees.

The right moment

Every business has a sweet spot when everything is going well, if not perfectly. Then there's an arc and an inevitable downswing. Sometimes a business dies of attrition when its owner and guiding force gets tired and shows up less—sometimes physically, sometimes just emotionally.

The whole point of starting a business is to grow that business, put in a huge amount of effort, and be compensated for all that effort.

Once you decide to sell you have to realize why you are getting out. For me, I knew I couldn't get past the current revenue mark on my own, so I put the company on the market.

I can't emphasize enough how you should plan to sell your firm from Day One in order to achieve greater profits. After the five year mark, the growth trajectory was going strong for me. I missed that mark because, like most business owners, I was wrapped up in the success we were achieving.

Remember this truth: When you love it the most is when you need to sell it.

Sales process

Sell a company when you're in love with it. Really?

Running a business is so much fun in the beginning, but inevitably that will change. Don't become too attached; keep emotion out of the equation. Start a company to sell and don't get wrapped up in its success.

When I watch *Shark Tank* or *The Profit*, which I do fairly often, I'm cognizant of the entrepreneur who is so wedded to his own story, the name and everything about it, that he misses the opportunity to make a deal, to increase profits exponentially—with the right help.

It's vital to know how much your business is worth. Determining its value depends upon realistically assessing costs, the market, the difficulty of obtaining and retaining customers, and actual and projected profits.

Too often selling or not selling is an emotional rather than a financial decision. When everyone is signing contracts and money is flowing—that is an optimum time to sell. But like timing the buying and selling of stocks so you buy at an absolute low and sell at an all-time high, positioning a company for sale at just the best moment for financial gain is a miracle. But doing so at a decent time is certainly achievable.

Downside of staying on after the sale

If your sales agreement includes a clause wherein you'll stay on for awhile, it's likely you'll soon feel like you're "doing time." In my case, the first six months were fine. Everyone was full of optimism and new opportunities. Then the reality hit that I had to work with managers who had opinions and methods of operating quite different from my own.

After all, I was no longer the owner and no longer in charge. I started counting the months until I was done. At the same time, I was mourning the loss of my business. It was strange to simultaneously want out and want to have it all back.

I thought I could walk away without being emotionally attached and was surprised how much I missed having "my company."

Always plan your exit well in advance.

Gains and losses

While the company was not a child and it was my decision to sell, and in spite of the fact I made millions on the transaction, not having my "baby" anymore is a loss. Though its sale opens up new and exciting opportunities for me, I miss it. It's harder to let go than I anticipated.

I also temporarily lost the title of CEO and with it, a piece of my identity. That's part of the reason I'm working on my next chapter. The other reason is that I love working and accomplishing something.

One thing I've learned through the ups and downs of my life is the necessity of moving forward. You can only look back for so long before stumbling on the road ahead. Take a mental picture, capture it in your mind, keep the lessons and the triumphs and yes, the failures, in your wheelhouse. And move on.

It's also a good idea to realize why you are getting out. Once you hit a certain revenue mark, once your industry is changing in a way that does not benefit your business, once it is no longer as challenging, after your growth trajectory reaches its peak, or when there's something else you'd rather be doing—getting out is a win. Making a large profit *is* a good reason. After all, that is the ultimate goal.

Just as running a business was done my way, choosing when and how to exit was important to do on my own terms, not on someone else's.

Lifestyle business

When I was getting ready to sell my company, the new owners kept referring to my business as a "lifestyle business"—as though that was a negative.

Apparently this was their view because I never grew the company past a certain revenue mark—I was happy keeping it at a certain size, just large enough to support my lifestyle and that of my partner. Because of this, the new owners judged it a lifestyle business.

My former business partner and I talked about this recently and we decided that having a "lifestyle business" was actually a positive thing. We worked as much as we wanted, treated everyone with respect, put our employees first, and paid ourselves what we're worth. We did take dips in pay to keep the business positive at times, but we created a business that worked for our lifestyle.

I would start another "lifestyle business" any day of the week.

It's important not to let others make you feel bad about what type of business you build. If it works for you, that's all that matters.

Did I do the right thing?

If you've gotten this far and sold your business, you may be tempted to have regrets. This is the old "woulda-shoulda-coulda" notion of second-guessing ourselves.

DON'T DO IT!

Once you sell your business, don't rethink it. Don't think "if only" I held onto it a bit longer, or "if only" I got more money for it, or "if only" I did…whatever.

Don't dwell on it. After all, hindsight is supposedly 20-20. You can always look back and think you should have done better.

Remember that you've already done great. Could it have been greater? Perhaps, but maybe not. Maybe you did better than anyone else would have or could have done with the same set of parameters. You'll never know.

What you can influence is a positive view of what you accomplished and your belief in yourself. You'll need these for your next venture, so give yourself the proverbial pat on the back and move on. No doubt there's a new challenge for you to tackle. If not, you can create one.

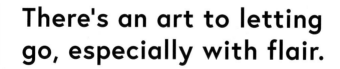

There's an art to letting go, especially with flair.

CHAPTER 14:

Winning and Losing

"The difference between winning and losing is most often not quitting."
—Walt Disney, extraordinary animator, entrepreneur, and film producer

Success

Success is measured different ways. There's money, of course, and there's also health, happiness and relationships. I've observed too many who work just to make money and then wonder, "What now?"

I have lots of friends who have money but it's sad that many of them are never satisfied. Money is only one piece, just a fraction of what we all need. Oh sure, it gives us financial security. But it doesn't provide someone to go to the movies with you, or the confidence to go yourself and not feel self-conscious. That's success too—to go to a spa, to lunch, and to enjoy it as an individual. It's success not to need someone else for validation.

I consider myself a winner if I'm comfortable with silence, perhaps reading a book or taking pictures with a camera to amuse myself. It's vital to like yourself. Too many people I've seen are always looking to move around and change jobs. What some don't realize is that however much you move around, you are still you. You can get distracted by the changes, which will keep you busy for awhile. But in the end, you go back to being you. If you're uncomfortable with that, you need to work on yourself.

One of my friends has a large savings plan, but lately she's been saying, "Now what?" She doesn't know the answer because as she says, "I've always worked." The work became her end goal. Her new goal is to travel and see more of the world once she has the time to enjoy it.

Curiosity, and thus lots of interests, is the key for those who succeed.

Staying happy

My husband and I have two homes—one in Big Sky, Montana, and the other in the Florida Keys. When we're not working, we live an outdoorsy, small town life. In Big Sky, there's skiing in the winter; and there's trout fishing (I've not tried this yet), white water rafting, and hiking in the summertime. Our house also sits on a golf course. I play, but I'm not very good.

I love decorating houses and remodeling too, so I usually have a project going at one of our houses.

In Florida, we go scuba diving, swimming, and boating. When we're there, we live in flip-flops and shorts so between our two homes, we have the best of both worlds.

I wouldn't want to live in the Keys full-time, for you get the island fever and don't want to do anything. When we moved there I had to adjust, for the people are laid-back and operating on island time.

When we first got there, I was one of the only ones working among my neighbors. Everyone else spent their time at happy hour, or on a boat or lobster fishing. For me, it was hard to be around so many people operating strictly on their own schedules.

Living there part-time does let me decompress. It's impossible not to go a little slower.

Adapting

Prior to selling my business, the plan was that I would run the business remotely.

When we got to the Florida Keys, it was beautiful out and I continued to dress in business clothes like I had in Seattle. I rented an office on the highway and went there every day—it was just me and I took along our two dogs. The ocean was crystal blue and the weather was glorious. There I was in my office while everyone else was outside enjoying themselves.

I was trying to bring my life, and how to do business in Seattle, to the Keys. I quickly realized I had to leave Seattle in the Northwest. Though I literally had no idea how to go about it, I made up my mind it was necessary.

Everyone in the Keys wears shorts and T-shirts. I thought, "I can't do that. But I can wear sundresses and sun hats—that's closer." I re-dressed myself so I no longer stuck out like a sore thumb. I traded my high heels and boots for flip-flops and sandals.

Meanwhile, the neighbors were all going to happy hour while I worked. My husband and I joined a bocce ball league—sort of an outdoor Italian bowling game. Pretty soon I was kicked off the team for not being gung-ho when I failed to attend daily practices. To the others, I obviously didn't take the game seriously enough. I wasn't totally kicked off—that's not the style in the Keys. I still play on the league but I'm relegated to the position of an alternate instead of as a regular.

I continued to have to work, so while others were playing—whether it was bocce ball or scuba diving or drinking—I was in the rented office on the highway. And I was miserable.

Then I had an epiphany—"Why am I fighting this?" I wondered. I was being dragged to happy hour and bocce ball.

Obviously I needed an attitude adjustment if I was going to acclimate to this new culture. Once I did this, I was happier and more comfortable all around.

The Florida Keys

My husband chose the Keys for us originally. We went on vacation numerous times to different islands and the Keys just spoke to him.

Island life was already on our radar screen. My Mum died when she was 53 and I'm in my fifties now. When I hit 53 I asked myself, "Am I doing everything I want to do if this is the last year of my life?" I always dreamed of going back to a beach resort because I worked in one as a kid and loved it.

Step one was figuring out what to wear as I described above. Step two was opening an office outside our home. My husband was fine working from the house, but I didn't work well sharing an office with my husband. So my dogs—Elliot, a Chihuahua mix, and Rainey, a German Shepherd—were my co-workers and daytime companions.

It soon became apparent we needed to sell the company. We could maintain the business long distance but being so far away would not facilitate our growing it. And I was becoming resentful of my husband enjoying happy hours and scuba diving while I worked in the office on the highway. My resentment wasn't fair to either of us.

Making a difference

It's a cliché, but those to whom life is generous should give back to benefit whatever causes they find themselves passionate about.

For me that would be helping animals who have no voice to help themselves.

In Seattle, I volunteered for a safe haven animal sanctuary that cares for abused farm animals. I cleaned out stalls and did whatever manual labor was needed. In the process, I decompressed from the physical activity and I love animals, so I felt good about what I was doing.

I believe in giving sweat equity as well as donating funds. Anyone can write a check and it's harder to give time. I do both, volunteering about 200 hours a year, which I think is a lot.

My husband is philanthropic too. He's Executive Director for Dive N2 Life, an organization that helps kids interested in STEM learn about science and issues like coral restoration. The whole family is involved in the organization, which is the brainchild of Kama and Richie Cannon. My stepson is the president and a dive instructor; and I volunteer by attending events. Thomas Troisch created the nonprofit's logo.

At Christmastime, I do whatever I can to support military families. They support us year-round, so it's the least we can do to make their holidays brighter. I usually sponsor several families by sending gift cards so they can choose what gifts to buy their own loved ones.

One year during the holidays, I was driving to a meeting with a new salesman on my team. When we were stopped at a light, there was a veteran outside and his dog was shivering. I rolled down the window and handed the veteran a blanket that was in my back seat. The salesman was especially touched because he is a veteran and dog lover.

To me, that's the true meaning of giving—you just do it without any fuss.

Competition

I think about winning and losing all the time. To me, losing is when I don't bring in any new contracts for a month. I love doing business development and landing a piece of business is the best reward.

At times when I lose to a competitor, I feel like a big loser and I focus on not having done enough. Then the next month when I land new business, I think, "Oh good."

My work in business is dependent on me making sure it's profitable. If it's not working, I come up with the answers. My husband says I'm most creative when I'm down. "That's when you get clever," he tells me. That's the same as when my Dad says I don't put my head in the sand. Instead I turn my head sideways to see what's around that I missed.

Striving for different goals

At first, I had a hard time comprehending why a woman I knew did not jump at a great job offer I obtained for her. Then I realized that not everyone has the same goals. To her, being successful meant working outside and not being stuck in an office.

Initially, I could not understand why she would not just go for it, but I learned to appreciate the differences among us. Not everyone is a risk-taker, nor do they have to be. What's important is we all find our own path.

Of course, whatever we try is not always going to work out. Just like playing the lottery, it is really hard to win when you never buy a ticket. The odds are against you, but guess what—eventually someone wins, someone beats the odds. It might as well be you.

Moving forward

Second guessing, looking in the rear view mirror, Monday morning quarterbacking, and other analyses with the benefit of hindsight are not my *modus operandi*. After all, you can only do the best you can do with the information you have on hand.

We all have the same amount of time in life. There are 24 hours in a day for each of us. It doesn't matter how much money you have, you can't buy more hours. And money can't fix what's broken regarding time and how it's spent.

No matter how many years you live, it's a relatively short amount of time in my opinion. I no longer believe in wasting a minute.

That's not to say that I believe in working all the time—quite the contrary. I believe in balancing work and leisure. Then there's the time that we do nothing much—just regrouping while we find time to think. It's amazing what we can think of when we're not trying. Our minds work well when they're not under pressure. If you believe in yourself, answers and creative solutions will come.

Never underestimate the damage that can derive from stress either; so as much as possible, take things in stride. Your health may well depend on it. If customers are demanding, do what you can to assist them.

But of course, someone else's bad planning shouldn't constitute an emergency for you.

If it's not your monkey, it's not your circus.

You can't win them all. Just be sure to enjoy the ride.

AFTERWORD

Whatever your wishes and dreams, take my advice and strive to obtain them. After all, it is not our failures that haunt us, but rather it's those attempts we choose not to make.

Self-sabotage is a wicked adversary. But self-confidence, supportive members of a team, and determination can and will allow you to persevere, translating into winning.

Winning, of course, takes different forms. But whatever that looks like for you, it is only attainable if you "go for it." So don't waste a second.

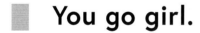 **You go girl.**

ACKNOWLEDGMENTS

One person stands out above all others for his endless support—my husband, Rex. He is an amazing dreamer and producer of great ideas. I became his partner in crime years ago; together we execute our plans and put them into motion.

Rex is a risk-taker who taught me not to hide in the shadows, but instead to let the sun hit right in my face. He likes to be referred to as a trophy husband at all the women's events I attend. That's because he knows his worth and is confident we are in a true partnership. Making fun of his role is just one of the ways he lets me shine.

Rex initially convinced me to quit my career in corporate America and open my own company. He continues to play the best supporting role I could ask for in a business partner, co-founder and best friend. He understands me and knows how to love a woman who has a hard external shell but is soft as can be inside.

I've always admired my brother, Steven, for his skill, persistence, and work ethic. Steven sets the bar high. No matter how busy he finds himself, he is always accessible to me for career and personal advice that I value and trust. He is my go-to person when things are tough.

My dad, Paul, has been my cheerleader from the start and I would not be the person I am today without his continued and ongoing support. My mum, Ann, was a truly influential and inspiring part of my life. I wish she were here to see her bravery in action through me. I am lucky my three aunts—Margaret, Irene, and

Kathleen—stepped up where she left off. Plus I have a wonderful stepmother, Elizabeth, who brought my dad happiness again.

My stepson, Jake, has a wickedly funny sense of humor and I am fortunate to spend so much time with him. Like his dad, he makes me laugh and helps me take life less seriously. My nephew, Dustin, was instrumental in getting our house in order after it was hit with major hurricane damage, and Dustin is entertaining to have around. My ever-supportive mother-in-law, Phyllis, deserves thanks for making sure I am not taking on too much. She is always the first to ask if I need anything.

My friend, Sanjay Rajashekar, came into my life as a business acquaintance and then as my friend when we were positioning my business for sale, showing me how to put my best foot forward. He always wants me to have a seat at the table. It is because of Sanjay that I was invited to transition into the boardroom of my former company. His M&A firm, aYatti, facilitated the sale of my business. Sanjay is father to a young lady who will blossom into an incredible entrepreneur if she takes after her dad. Plus, he has the support of a beautiful wife and partner Heather Goring, who is always looking for new opportunities for us to explore.

One special person has worked with me over the course of more than 20 years and I wish to thank him. Noland Angara has dotted every "i" and crossed every "t" for which I needed help. Without Noland's attention to detail, I would not have been as successful. He was a co-founder of my company and the backbone of my business.

I also want to acknowledge all the other great employees who worked at my company, Red Sky Blue Water, over the years—making the company a great place to work. I especially want to thank Thomas Troisch, Tauschia Copeland, Stephen Kamnetz, Mark Ferguson, Dawn Aldrich, Masha Bobrovskaya, Eleni Jimenez, Dana Brokaw, Tiffany Barnes, Erin Burke, Camille Crowell, Celeste

Combs, Robert Uhlenkott, Marissa Kaiser, Lea Lönnberg-Hickling, Nathan Cant, Michael Richardson, Kelli Vaz, Tres Cozine, Matt Karren, Grant Stalley, Ryan Charbonneau, Patrick Haberkamp, Sharmini Thamboo, Shomik Ghosh, Kayleigh Stalley, Israel Evans, and Matt Kalkoske.

Pieter Uittenbogaard, Paul Simpson, Puvi Thamboo, Alex Rublowsky, Tiffany Allesina, Liena Ugarova, Helen Harmetz, Gayna Williams, Nathan Kaiser, Michael Del Sarto, Steve Campbell, Katya Palladina, and Adrienne Curran are much appreciated for being amazing clients and friends over the span of the business.

I wish to thank iLink Systems Inc., the technology firm that bought my company, Red Sky. Thanks to iLink, I fulfilled the third part of my dream—Start, Build, and Sell. iLink gave my company freedom to keep its own identity and guidance to grow using their knowledge and resources. I am most grateful.

Finally my gratitude goes to my little rescue dog, Elliot, as he racked up frequent flyer miles traveling with me between Florida, Montana, and Washington State when I was selling my company and finishing out my commitment as CEO. During the transition, Elliot gained the honorary Viking name, Elliot Two Toes Missing, after a mishap on an airport escalator. Elliot is taking it in stride, which is my advice to budding entrepreneurs—don't sweat little stuff. In this case, the little stuff is two tips on a rear paw.

.

ABOUT THE AUTHOR

Sharon A. Davison, Ph.D. is a talented entrepreneur with a passion for business. She began her career designing innovative solutions in the field of human-computer interaction and usability. Sharon added strategic marketing, program management and communication to her toolbox and parlayed her expertise into building her own multimillion-dollar business, which she later sold for a substantial profit.

Sharon is an educator as well as a business owner and she has taught graduate level courses at the University of Seattle as an adjunct professor. She also delivers speeches and consults with business owners to guide them through the growth of their businesses.

Sharon has a Bachelor of Science in psychology and sociology, as well as a Master of Arts in experimental psychology. She also has a Ph.D. in experimental psychology with a concentration in human-computer interaction.

"I watch people and I observe them," Sharon explains. "I study how and why they interact with each other, how they use products, and what they do with technology. Understanding customers' motivations and desires will always come in handy when running a business."